THE BLESSED FRIEND
OF YOUTH

SAINT JOHN BOSCO

BY

NEIL BOYTON, S.J.

Second Revised Edition

NEW YORK
THE MACMILLAN COMPANY

Imprimi Potest:

    EDUARDUS C. PHILLIPS, S.J.,

        Præpositus Prov.

        Marylandiæ Neo-Eboracensis.

Imprimi Potest:

    RICHARDUS PITTINI, S.C.,

        Præpositus Prov.

Nihil Obstat:

    ARTHUS J. SCANLAN, S.T.D.

        Censor Librorum.

Imprimatur:

    ✠ PATRICK CARDINAL HAYES,

        Archbishop, New York.

New York, September 29, 1934.

Set up and electrotyped.

Published December, 1929.

Revised edition, October, 1934.

Reprinted January, 1935.

Second Revised Edition, November, 1942.

Reprinted April, 1943.   January, 1944.

SET UP BY BROWN BROTHERS LINOTYPERS

PRINTED IN THE UNITED STATES OF AMERICA

BY THE FERRIS PRINTING COMPANY

TO

SAINT DON BOSCO'S PRESENT AND FUTURE

AMERICAN SONS AND DAUGHTERS

CONTENTS

THE BLESSED FRIEND OF YOUTH
SAINT JOHN BOSCO

CHAPTER I

A CONQUEROR IS BORN

On August 16, 1815, a British warship was carrying a conqueror to a bleak island in the South Atlantic. There he was to be held, like some great eagle caged, till death came. This inhospitable island was St. Helena and the prisoner was he whom men called "The Little Corporal." Europe and America were following in imagination the last voyage of this prisoner. Some with relief in their hearts; some with sorrow; some with wounds of Waterloo still healing; some with widowed and orphaned bitterness. For such a conqueror leaves a trail of blood and woe, whether his ambition leads him to victory or defeat.

As glory was fading in the western skies that same evening of August 16, 1815, another babe was being born in a poor suburb of Turin, Italy. Thus unheralded was coming on the stage of life one who was destined to do greater things for his fellow men than Napoleon Bonaparte. The farmer folks in this poor suburb of Castelnuovo d'Asti—Becchi was its name—knew next day that a boy child had come to the humble home of Francis and Margaret Bosco. There were already two boys there; Anthony, who was Mrs. Bosco's stepson, and toddling two-year-old Joseph. Now the new baby.

Francis and Margaret pondered over a suitable name for their youngest and they hit upon a happy choice. For they called the baby after the boy apostle whom Jesus loved exceedingly. So a few days later in the parish church a new Child of God was held over the baptismal font and the pastor christened him John—John Melchior Bosco.

John Bosco never saw Napoleon. Yet both had traits in common. Both were conquerors in their chosen spheres. One looked on his world through the greedy eyes of an Alexander and for a few brief years satisfied the greed in his eyes. He became a Prince of the Apostles of Mars. But he built his empire on sand and the winds and the rains came and it passed away before he did. Six dreary years from his high prison he looked back on his broken life works. Please God, in those long months of exile and humiliation he saw his wasted ambition in its true light. When he went to render his account on that May evening in 1821 let us hope that a Merciful Judge had pity on his soul. Poor Napoleon Bonaparte!

Not so was it with John Bosco. He also was to be a conqueror. By the peaceful ways of Christ he was to become the Beloved Apostle of Youth. All the days of his long life he saw his world through the gentle eyes of Jesus and his dear Mary, Help of Christians. He also cherished high ambitions. He dreamed dreams and he saw them become splendid realities. Not to conquer men and bend them to his will was his life work. No mother ever cursed his name for leaving her son, pale and horrible, on some European battlefield. But many a mother brought her son to his side and many a motherless boy came to his shelter and there learned to bless the day that he had come under the influence of this Father of Orphans.

For John Bosco's earliest ambition was to lead the souls of boys to God. To further this consuming ambition he sacrificed what a blinded world calls everything. And when John Bosco came to the end of his full days he saw his ambition realized a hundredfold; he went before his Judge with the smile of a true conqueror on his lips. For what he had built was built on firm rock and it was built to increase and endure.

The honors that he avoided all his life crowded around that holy deathbed. Higher honors than he dared to hope for have come, and are coming, to his pleasant memory. When he died, men cried that a saint had gone to his reward. Legions of "Don Bosco's Boys" cherished his memory, for what they were they owed to his paternal love. His religious children—Salesian sons and daughters and coöperators—carry on his boy works on all continents to-day. The Sovereign Pontiff, Pius XI, speaking when the Decree on Don Bosco's heroic virtues was read in the Consistorial Hall of the Vatican, February 20, 1927, said:

> Don Bosco towers head and shoulders above the ordinary run of men; he is a gigantic figure upon whom Divine Providence has lavished its choicest gifts. We have seen this man—John Bosco—face to face; we have talked with him; we have examined his character and we have seen his profound humility he tried in vain to conceal; we have watched him in his daily life. . . . In our opinion, he was one of those men who leave the mark of their genius wherever they are. . . .

Rich John Bosco!

It is in the hope that the life of such a conqueror, who did his valiant deeds in the days of their fathers and their grandfathers, may be read with interest by good American boys that this biography of a modern man of God and friend of boys is attempted.

CHAPTER II

A HOLY CHILD

THE house in which John Bosco was born still stands in Becchi. Over here in America such a humble birth-place would be an invaluable asset for any presidential candidate. It is a two-story combination barn and home. Outside, sort of rickety fire-escape steps lead to the upper floor. A farmyard opens off the "front steps." Here hens held sway, forever pecking at some barnyard titbit. A small hillside farm stretched away its few acres and beyond was an orchard and vineyard. The country-side was valley and green-clad hills, through which the shaded roads of Piedmont ran in all directions. By day a Madonna-blue sky looked down.

These were the familiar sights baby John saw. His first recollections go back to these toddling days. Long afterwards Don Bosco wrote:

> I was not yet two years old, when my father died, and I cannot remember what he was like. I do not know how it affected me. I only remember that my mother said, "You have no father now"; and that is my earliest recollection.

To prove that he really did remember that far back, he added the details:

> As all the relatives went out of the room where my father lay I wanted to remain, but my mother took

10

me away. I still persisted, saying: "If father cannot come, neither shall I." But my mother replied: "Poor child, come with me. You have no father now." Then she burst into tears, took me by the hand and led me elsewhere, while I began to weep for no other reason than because Mama was weeping. For at that age I certainly could not understand what it meant to lose one's father. But I never forgot those words, "You have no father now."

It is recorded elsewhere that Francis Bosco, just before the end, beckoned his wife to his bedside and gave her two requests: "Be resigned to God's Holy Will" and "Take care of our boys, but of little John in a special manner."

That Mrs. Bosco, or Mama Margaret, as she came to be known with the years, heeded her dying husband's request, there is the clearest proof. Don Bosco had a good father, but he had a holy mother and, as has been the case in the making of all the worth-while men of the world, it was the influence of that holy mother that lifted the son to sanctity.

Early she began to plant the seed of the parable in this "good ground." We have preserved for us an incident, when John was but four years old. It was a hot summer day in 1819 and John and his older brother Joseph came into the house to get a drink. Mama Margaret took the mug from the table and, filling it with water, held it out to Joseph. Little John promptly took the smile off his face and replaced it with an unmistakable frown of jealousy at his mother's preference. When Joseph had drained the mug, the mother refilled it and offered it to her youngest. John shook his dark curls in refusal. Mama Margaret wisely said nothing, but emptied the water out and went about her household duties.

After a short while she felt a tug at her skirt and looking down saw John. Timidly he said: "Mama."

"Yes, son?"

"Give me a drink, too."

"I thought you were not thirsty?"

John hung his head and begged: "I'm sorry, Mama, I acted that way."

"Surely, dear. My little son knows I love him and Joseph equally well. Now tell Our dear Lord that you are sorry for anything that was wrong"; and with her invariable smile, "Here's your drink."

A wise woman that Mama Margaret!

In the childhood of John Bosco there are two mentions of "the rod in the corner." In Becchi there was no danger of spoiling the children by sparing it. But as in the case of the thoroughbred colt, for small John, the suggestion was more effective than the application.

For instance, John had been up to some childish misbehavior. Mama Margaret called the culprit and he came hesitatingly forward.

"John, do you see that rod in the corner?"

"Yes, Mama." John prudently retreated several steps.

"Well, go and get it and bring it to me."

Here John asked what we would call "a foolish question."

"What do you want to do with it, Mama?"

"Bring it to me and you will see."

Reluctantly John obeyed. Very gravely he asked: "Are you going to use it on me?"

"And why not, if you continue to act as you have been doing?"

John looked up, his dark eyes serious. "Please, Mama, I will stop it."

Mama Margaret knew her son's word was golden and smilingly she told him to restore the rod to its place in the corner.

That other mention of the rod was the day John's Grandmother Occhiena discovered some fruit, which she had carefully put away, was missing. Many a grandmother has made the same discovery and many a grandmother has leaped to the same conclusions that John's did. She accused the smallest of her grandsons of the theft. But she was wrong that time. John had not taken the fruit. So with a clean conscience he went as ordered and got the "rod in the corner." He happened to know his stepbrother, Anthony, was the one who had eaten the missing fruit. As ever, charitable-minded and wishing to save his brother a hiding, he offered: "Grandma, I didn't take your fruit, but if I tell you who did, will you forgive him and not lick him? Please, Grandma."

There must have been something extra appealing in the child's tones, for the old woman's lips softened and she promised: "Well, Johnnie, if he asks me to forgive him and brings the rod to show that he knows he has done something wrong, in taking what wasn't his, I'll do so this time."

John returned the rod to the corner and disappeared out of the room. Shortly after this, Anthony came in, went and got the rod and stood before his grandmother with downcast eyes. Again the rod was returned to the corner without being put "on active service."

Mama Margaret believed in the sensible plan of letting

her sons have pets and when the occasion offered, she used the pets to drive home suitable lessons. Once John had caught a young owl. Whatever name he gave it has not been recorded. But we do know he was devoted to his pet and kept it in the home. When the cherries were ripe, he bought a basket of the tempting fruit home and, first thing, offered his pet one. It was accepted without a display of manners, and fruit and stone disappeared. Then the greedy bird opened his beak and stretched out his neck to signal to his small master that more were wanted immediately. The owl got one. Then another and another. They only seemed to whet his appetite.

Finally, John, to whose tender mind Mama Margaret had already inculcated the virtue of temperance, grew impatient with his feathered pig of a pet and putting the whole basket of cherries alongside the owl, said in deep disgust: "Here, bird, take as many as you like. I'm tired of feeding you." And he walked off.

The young owl did not need a second invitation. But when John returned he was horrified to discover that his pet had choked itself to death on the cherries. John carried the dead bird to his mother, who took the swollen body and holding it out, said: "My son, look at the end of gluttons! In beast or man, nothing hastens death more than gluttony and intemperance. Take your greedy owl away and bury him in the corner of the orchard."

That one object lesson on the virtue of temperance John Bosco never forgot and often he retold the anecdote to his boys.

Then there was that other pet of the Bosco household, a large dog. Mama Margaret had gotten him as a pup;

and when she married Francis Bosco, the dog came to the new home. Somewhat like Nana in *Peter Pan*, this big shaggy dog was watchman of the farm and household by night and pal and guardian of the children by day.

Grandfather and Grandmother Occhiena wanted a dog and Mama Margaret decided to give them hers. So she took him to her parent's farm and left him there. But the dog did not care to be a party to the transfer of ownership. He trotted back to Becchi and into the Bosco yard. Not sure of his welcome he advanced with head and tail down. Mama Margaret gave him no pat on the head and the big dog, enveloped in gloom, slunk across to his accustomed corner and lay down. A ray of hope! At least, he was not ordered out! The children were delighted that their big shaggy companion was back. But the grandparents wanted that dog, so they came for him. Too quietly he let them lead him back to their farm. Then, waiting his chance, he bit through his rope and hiked back to the Bosco hearth.

Anthony met him with menacing stick. The dog crouched low and as the boy approached, he turned over, and with paws at prayer, begged and begged and begged that he might be allowed to stay. In the meantime, Mama Margaret, Joseph and John had come out to witness the return of the runaway, or the prodigal canine, depending on the point of view. Little John was not opposed to his pal's return.

The dog's submission to any licking that was coming to him, provided only that he might be allowed to stay in the Bosco home, won the day. Anthony lowered his stick and joined his brothers in an eloquent plea to Mama Margaret.

Finally, she capitulated. "It looks as though we will have to get Grandmother and Grandfather another watch dog. This bad, bad fellow," the dog crouched lower and lower at Mama Margaret's feet, "may stay."

She turned to the three boys and remarked: "Look, my children, what patience, submission, and affection he shows toward us, to whom he is merely indebted for a drink of water and some scraps of food!" And making the most of her opportunity, she added: "Ah, my little ones, would that we were even half as grateful to God, to Whom we owe everything; not only this world's goods, but a soul created to His image and destined to live forever in His Kingdom!"

The large dog remained on the farm for a few years, but Mama Margaret's wise words remained in the heart of her smallest son indelibly.

Like all barefooted boys John early in his days developed a love for the fields, and his young heart was one with the gentle St. Francis of Assisi, for he also loved the birds. He knew where they nested and many a fistful of crumbs was carried from the table to feed some particular favorites.

We do not know how old John was when this next incident happened. One sunny afternoon he was in the fields and he chanced on a nightingale's nest. John carefully marked its location and he used to return whenever he had the opportunity to watch the mother hatching her eggs. Then came the glad day when he was able to tell Mama Margaret that the fledglings were hatched. More crumbs left the table in John's fist. The mother bird got to know him and permitted him to come close to her hungry youngsters.

But a common tragedy was near and John was unfortunate enough to witness it. While he was silently occupied in what an American boy scout would call, "working for his merit badge in bird study," a large cuckoo landed on a branch close to the nest. The European cuckoo is blood brother to our blue jay—the ruthless "gunman" among the feathery brethren.

The cuckoo with wings outspread pounced on the brave mother. She put up what fight she could for her fledglings, but was quickly overcome. Then the victorious cuckoo killed and ate the fledgings, too! Little John, watching, horrified, from the shelter of his "observation post," saw tiny feathers floating down and was unable to avert the wholesale murders. Tears welled up in his eyes. He was angry, too, for he looked on these little nightingales as his friends of the fields. But when he had dried his eyes on the sleeve of his shirt, he saw that the murder-minded cuckoo had killed the nightingale family to get their nest for her own young. She dropt down to the ground, laid an egg and seizing it in her beak, flew back to the pilfered nest.

The avian melodrama was not over. Retributive justice in the form of a sly cat appeared on the stage. Silently as any wild animal on the hunt, the cat crept closer and closer. His tail, whipped to and fro as he advanced, till he was able to spring and grasp the cuckoo. The cat finished his supper in a few mouthfuls and the watching boy must have smiled his approval at the passing of the cuckoo to that place from which no cuckoo ever returns.

Little John had a tale of murder and justice to tell at the family supper table that night. But he was not through with the adventure yet. Next time he was in the vicinity of the tiny tragedy he discovered that a foolish nightingale had found the orphaned cuckoo egg and was mothering it. In due time the cuckoo was hatched out and still its foster mother fed it.

John knew more of the ways of cuckoos than that simple-minded nightingale did. He guessed rightly the time would shortly come when the young cuckoo would be old enough to turn on its foster mother and dine on her in return for her care. So he made a small cage and he caught the cuckoo. Back to the Bosco farm he brought his captive. Boylike he fed it regularly for some days. Then boylike his mind became busied with other things.

Mama Margaret found the starved baby cuckoo in the bottom of its cage. She went to the door and called: "Johnnie, O Johnnie, come here."

He came and she asked: "When did you feed that young cuckoo last?"

The answer flushed in his shamed countenance. He ran across to the cage. That particular cuckoo would require no future feeding.

"Little son," Mama Margaret detained John by the side of the cage, "If it was the big dog now, who died of starvation, you'd weep. But I notice no tears in your eyes." She went on to recall the fate of the mother cuckoo and the imprudence of the nightingale mother in hatching a strange egg. "And now he suffers for the sins of his tribe. Always remember, little son, the property of others is not yours to take. That cuckoo had no right to the nightingale's nest and it paid dearly for its theft. Another thing to thank God for, is the happiness of having good parents. If this had been a baby nightingale, I am sure you would have loved it enough to have cared faithfully for it. But it belonged to parents who have a bad reputation and so it paid the penalty. You, my son, should thank God daily for having had such a good father."

Quickly John smiled up in her face and replied: "Yes; but I thank Him more for having given me you for a mother."

And he was off to tend his cow. This was John's first job. Joseph had had it, but when his young brother was old enough to take charge, he became the family cow-tender.

John would take his charge to the field in the early morning. Here he had a companion of his own age. Poor as the Boscos were, this lad came from a poorer family. The difference was noticeable in the quality of bread each boy brought along for his breakfast. The boy's was dark unpalatable stuff, while Mama Margaret gave John a piece of white bread.

The other boy would cast envious eyes on that finer bread. One day John said to him: "Will you do me a favor?"

"Sure. What is it?" questioned the boy.

"Change bread with me. Your bread must be better than mine and I like it better."

Gladly was the exchange made and it became a frequent occurrence. It was not till years after that the boy understood that John was practicing a little act of daily mortification.

Such are some of the anecdotes that have been preserved for us of the childhood of John Bosco. Easily we can see behind them the influence of that holy mother, whose constant care was to instill in the hearts of her boys the thought of God. If she had any motto before her

eyes in this education, it was "God sees you." This she
kept repeating to them. To her youngest, she taught it
with his first prayers. These, by the way, he learnt to
recite before Joseph, who was two years his senior.

This motto, "God sees you," she would whisper to
John when he would go to the neighboring fields to play.
If there had been a boyish disagreement, and they happen
in the saintly households as well as at the more normal
hearths, she would take the children aside and tell them:
"Remember that God sees you and knows also your most
secret thoughts." If there was a question of using "the
rod in the corner" and she saw the temptation to shield
themselves behind a—well, call it a light gray lie—"God
sees you and reads your hearts" would usually bring a
frank confession of the fault.

Again this wonderful Mama Margaret, who never learned
to read or write, would take her youngest out into the
barnyard on a starry night. Pointing to those points of
light that were distant worlds, she would tell her silent
boy, who gazed with upturned countenance, that God
had created them. How powerful must the great God be!
Into the fields in flowery spring, into the gathering clouds
of a summer storm, into the colorful autumn harvest,
Mama Margaret would read the beauty and the power
and the fatherliness of God.

She made the woods and the meadows and the skies a
vivid catechism from which she gave John his early religious instruction. So it is no wonder that this child, who
was destined to do great things for the Good God, listened
and learnt and absorbed the love of the God Who saw
him always.

Mama Margaret herself prepared John for his First
Confession and when he was old enough, she took him to

the parish church and there John Bosco received his second Sacrament. Some of the village folk who saw the innocent-eyed lad at this period of his boyhood, remarked to Mama Margaret: "You are fortunate to have such a good son. He is like an angel."

CHAPTER III

A BOY WHO SPOKE OF GOD

DESPITE the early manifestation of a deep spirituality John had his run of the usual boyhood adventure. There was one memorable ghost story he used to retell with relish. With his Mama Margaret he had gone to some cousins' home to help gather in the grapes at vintage time. In the evening, with the family seated at the table, the conversation turned to the weird. Like the rest, John, who was the youngest present, sat open-mouthed while his cousin told of strange noises that recently he himself had heard coming from the very garret overhead.

"It must have been the devil walking there," some cousin with a vivid imagination whispered. "That was his tail and his chains dragging!"

John, who knew his catechism as well as anyone in the room, spoke out: "Devil, nothing! It was something that happened naturally and I'll bet you, too."

The pitying looks of the circle of listeners denied the child's assertion. As if in proof of this almost universal doubt, there was a crash overhead. All were on their feet; John included in the risers. Evidently the devil was out for another stroll through the garret. The sound was repeated with a crash as of bricks falling. Then a dragging sound right across the floor above! It was very quiet in that family circle and panic was nigh. Even Mama Margaret was willing to admit it might be a walking devil. She reached for her treasure and putting her hand on John's shoulder, said: "Let us get out."

But John of the pure conscience had the strength of ten. He objected: "No; don't run away, Mama. I want to see what is making that noise."

Again the dragging sound was heard distinctly overhead. All were wishing devoutly that they had been talking of other subjects when this happened.

John lifted the lamp up from the table and invited: "Let us see what is the trouble up there."

It seemed at first as if he would go seeking the trouble alone. He climbed the wooden stairs that led into the garret. But his courage was contagious. More lamps and candles were lit, while sticks were grasped in case . . . John opened the trapdoor and raised his light on high. The shadows retreated and displayed a silent, disordered, dust-laden garret, with a corn sieve in the middle of the floor. The others were peering over John's shoulder when the sieve partially raised itself and began a stroll directly at the frightened group. That was too much for taut nerves. There was a general scramble down the wooden stairs.

John and a stout-hearted cousin were left alone. With steady hand he passed the lamp to this cousin and took several steps toward the sieve. It also advanced to the meeting. This was too much for the cousin. He dropt the lamp with a crash and fell into the agitated bosom of his family downstairs.

John shouted from the dark: "Give me a light!"

With trembling hands it was passed up to him and he set it on a broken-down chair. Then stooping over he put hands to the sieve.

"Don't touch it!" he was warned. But John picked up

the sieve. The cousins peering in from the head of the stairs broke out into a relieved laughter. There was an old hen who had flown into the garret through a broken window and by her pecking at the grains of corn left in the wiring, trapped herself when the sieve fell over on her. No wonder there had been strange noises lately in that garret!

We wonder if there were any more ghost stories retold the rest of that evening? Or was John's courage praised to his evident discomfort?

At another vintage time of his boyhood his courage was put to the test. This time there had been a poor yield of grapes and Mama Margaret heard that robbers were stealing her small crop. One afternoon she noticed a stranger lurking about, studying her grapevines. She suspected his purpose. Gathering together Anthony, Joseph, and John, she directed them to hide in the vineyard and not to show themselves till she shouted. Mama Margaret herself, as soon as it was dark, took up her position and joined the watch. After an hour or so the family vigil was rewarded. Mama Margaret detected a dark figure moving about and cutting off some of her bunches of grapes.

She stept out of her concealment and asked the man what he was doing in her vineyard. When the intruder saw that it was a woman addressing him, he struck at her. At once she shouted: "Robbers! Robbers!" Almost as an echo came the same cry from various parts of the dark vineyard. This was more than the thief had reckoned on and leaving his basket, he fled at breakneck speed out of that too-well-guarded vineyard.

The boys gathered around their mother and listened to her comment. "My sons, see how weak and frightened bad conscience leaves a man! We needed no pistols to put such a coward to flight."

She must have noticed how her words were eagerly listened to by her youngest, for she added: "This bad man could steal only our fruit, which at the most is not of great value, but you, sons, possess a precious treasure. I mean, your innocence. Beware that bad boys whom you may meet on your journey through life do not through your inexperience steal that away from you."

The children nodded their realization of this home-made lesson. So they left the vineyard and all trooped back to the house and bed.

Wise Mama Margaret often warned her sons against companions who might not have their tenderness of conscience.

John from his earliest years was on his guard. Even, in this respect, when he was the guardian of the family cow. But this constant watchfulness did not make him shun his young companions. Rather, boys attracted him in those days as they did all through his long, fruitful adult life.

We have recorded the incident of those early days when he tended the family cow in the meadows below Becchi. Other hamlet boys also watched their family supply of milk. Naturally, these "cow boys" congregated; sometimes to the neglect of their charges.

John liked to say his rosary. It was his constant companion. His was the first ear to catch the sounds of the Angelus bell, and he would kneel down wherever he was and say his prayer to his heavenly Mother.

But sometimes everything in that meadow was not so peaceful. One evening John led his cow home and Mama Margaret was quick to notice that there was a gash in her son's head. Rightly she blamed it on one of the other youthful cow tenders. She complained: "Why do you go with such bad boys?"

"That is just why I go with them," John answered. "If I am with them, they are better and do not say bad words."

"Yet you come home with a broken head!" With motherly concern she bathed and bandaged that gash.

John explained: "It was an accident."

"You must not go with them any more."

"Mama . . ." John could plead with the appeal of a winsome youngster.

"You've heard what I said."

"But, Mama, if it is to please you, I shall not go with them any more. But when I am with them, they do as I want them to do and do not fight any more."

John knew his Mama Margaret and he waited, smiling up at her. Finally she withdrew her prohibition and was rewarded with an affectionate kiss.

It was about this period that John had his remarkable dream. Remarkable it was, for it forecasted most accurately his apostolate for boy work. Years later, at the command of the then reigning Pontiff, Pius IX, Don Bosco wrote out this dream. We can do no better than quote his own words.

> At the age of about nine years I had a dream which remained deeply impressed upon my mind for the rest of my life. In the dream I seemed to be near a house in a large courtyard, where a crowd of boys were gathered together. Some were laughing, others playing, and many among them blaspheming.
>
> On hearing these blasphemies, I immediately rushed into their midst, raising my voice and using my fists to make them keep quiet.

One wonders, reading this, if this is an explanation of that recent gash?

Don Bosco continued:

> At that moment a dignified-looking man, who seemed to be in the prime of life and was nobly clad, appeared on the scene. A white mantle covered the whole of His person; but His face was so radiant that I was unable to look at it for long. He called me by name, and directed me to place myself at the head of these boys, concluding with these words, "You must win the hearts of these friends of yours, not with blows, but with sweetness and charity. Set to work at once then to instruct them on the wickedness of sin and on the excellence of virtue."
>
> While He was speaking all the boys had stopped fighting, shouting and blaspheming, and had gathered around the Stranger. Confused and somewhat afraid, I told Him that I was a poor and ignorant child, wholly unfitted to speak of religion to others. Almost without knowing what I was saying, I asked: "Who are You Who commands me to do what is impossible?"
>
> "Precisely because these things seem impossible to you, you must make them possible by obedience and by the acquisition of knowledge."
>
> "But where and how can I acquire this knowledge?"
>
> "I shall give you a Mistress under whose guidance you will become wise, and without whom all learning is mere foolishness."
>
> "But who are You to speak to me in this way?"

"I am the Son of Her whom your mother taught you to salute three times a day."

"My mother forbids me to mix with strangers without her permission, so tell me your name please?"

"Ask my Mother what My name is."

At that moment I saw at His side a Lady of majestic bearing, clothed in a mantle which shed a bright light all around, as if every point on it were a brilliant star. Seeing that I became more and more confused in my questions and replies, He motioned me to go near Her. Taking me kindly by the hand, She said, "Look, dear." And turning around, I noticed that all the boys had disappeared and in their stead I beheld a herd of goats, dogs, cats, bears, and other animals.

"This is your field of labor; this is where you must work," continued the Lady. "Make yourself humble, determined and strong. You must do for my sons what you will now see happen to these animals."

I then looked again, and to my surprise, instead of fierce animals, I now saw gentle lambs, all frisking about and bleating merrily, as if to do honor to the Man and the Lady.

At this point of the dream I commenced to cry and begged the Lady to speak clearly, because I did not know what all these things meant. She then put Her hand on my head and said: "In good time, my son, you will understand everything."

Naturally, John's dream was the subject of the breakfast table talk. When he had repeated it, the family made frank comment.

"I guess that means you are going to be a shepherd of goats and sheep," said practical Joseph.

Anthony, the stepbrother, who always seemed to be jealous of John, remarked sneeringly: "Well, I hope it does not mean you will become a chief of brigands some of these days."

We can see the reproving look Mama Margaret gave the eldest son.

Grandmother Occhiena thought it a good opportunity to tell the boy not to pay attention to dreams. But Mama Margaret, who knew this dreamer of hers better than anyone in the world, smiled and spoke in her turn: "Who knows but this may mean that some day my Johnnie will be a priest of God."

She it was who first put her finger unerringly on the secret longing of this boy.

Mama Margaret after this, gave more time to preparing John for his First Holy Communion. She took her lad to the parish priest and when he had examined John he was surprised to learn the extent of holy knowledge that John possessed. Unlike the Doctors in the Temple, this discerning Levite saw the child's worth and readiness, and made John very happy by telling him he would be permitted to make his First Holy Communion at the approaching Easter. This was in 1826 and John was about ten and a half. The usual age for children to receive Our Lord in those days before Early First Communion was at fourteen. So a big exception was made, and wisely made, in favor of this youthful rival of St. Aloysius.

The coming of Our Lord brought visible results in this fine youngster. He was different from other innocent boys. You have all met and been attracted to boys whose innocence is something tangible and elevating. This attractiveness was most noticeable in young John Bosco. One of the confidences of those days has been recorded. With the loving mother's unerring instinct, Mama Margaret brought up the subject of life work and John said: "Mama, if I can one day be a priest, I will consecrate my whole life to boys. I want to attract them to myself. I will love them and will make myself loved by them. I will give them good advice, for I do want to live for the salvation of their souls."

Words of rare maturity from a boy not yet entered into his teens and words that show a definite longing for that particular sphere of influence in which the memory of Don Bosco is singularly hallowed.

A whole chapter could be given to the early working out of this youthful apostolate. John had a more retentive memory than is usual. It held on to any edifying anecdote or incident like a vise. From Mama Margaret he heard tales of the angels and the saints and these he would retell to his fellow cow tenders and later to the other boys of the hamlet.

Soon John's gift of story telling was known in the younger circles of Becchi and he was always sure of an appreciative audience. John Bosco would have made a fine showman, for he had the Barnum and the Rickard knack of appreciating the worth of the ballyhoo.

Around Becchi were several small towns and the big events there were fair days and market days. Many a time Mama Margaret and John hiked to the neighboring towns. The mother to dispose of some farm produce or stock; John for the purpose of studying the traveling show folks. When he elbowed his way through a crowd of villagers around a troupe of acrobats and magicians, John secured a "ringside" position to study the tumbles and sleight of

hand tricks of the performers. We have been able to
unearth only a few of the tricks that the watchful-eyed
John carried back to Becchi with him, but it is easy to
reconstruct some of them. You see the acrobats every
year when the Ringling Brothers and Barnum and Bailey
Circus come to your home town, and the tumbles of the
clowns and performers are similar to the ones John practiced and mastered.

The sleight of hand secrets that John discovered on fair
and market days were card tricks, palming cards, produc-
ing small eggs and coins from the hats and even from the
elbows and knees of the wide-eyed boy subjects. John
even attempted tight-rope walking after seeing it at a
neighboring fair.

But the public performance of all these show-world acts
in the pleasant meadow below Becchi was only the ballyhoo—the showman's bait thrown out to attract the crowd.
"Step up closer, ladies and gentlemen," we can almost
hear John imitating the barker. And when the youthful
mob did, John would halt his free show and standing on a
chair say, "Let us recite Our Lady's rosary." That was the
price of admission and it was gladly paid by the audience.

John had too good a showman's instinct to deceive his
public. At that early stage of his career he had never
heard of the American master showman, who is credited
with the saying, "A fool is born every minute." He mixed
his boyish piety with circus stunts and he held his audience
and sent them away eager to return another day. For,
always after the beads had been said, the pious John Bosco
would step down and turn showman. He would back
somersault, walk on his hands, twist and tumble.

Then would come a return to pious practices. John
would mount his chair and say: "All you boys and girls

join in a hymn to Our Lady." He would lead off and at the Marian song's conclusion he would retell one of his anecdotes or announce. "Before I start the best part of my performance, I am going to tell you what the curate at Murialdo said in church last Sunday."

Some of his hearers would laugh and grumble at the thought of a sermon; others would start to move away, but John always had an ace in his hand. For he would announce grandly: "All right, you fellows can go out of the meadow if you wish, but, remember, you can't return to watch the new tricks I am going to show that I learned at the last fair."

The boy would point to the table, heaped high with mysterious properties. Very few left. Soon they would lose themselves listening to the boy preacher. At the end of his sermon, John would faithfully start the next part of his performance without delay.

This usually consisted of conjuror's tricks. John, after the manner of the Italian strolling performers, would strap a small knapsack to his back. Breathlessly would he be watched by his child audience. He would step up to an unsuspecting boy, show a coin, palm it in approved style and while the mystified boy would watch, he would pass to another boy and take the missing coin out of that one's ear. Again he would juggle three or four balls at once. This was followed by the trick of filling a glass with water, covering it and when he switched off the cloth, lo! there was a glass brimful of red wine!

But the big attraction was, showmanlike, kept for the climax. This was the trick called "killing the cock." John would produce a live cock from his knapsack, sharpen his knife loudly, and proceed to cut the fowl into pieces. When he had satisfied his audience that the cock was dead, John would gather up the parts, cover them, and then amidst a breathless silence, he would remove the cloth and there would be a very much alive cock. John would throw him on the ground where the cock, delighted to be released from dark confinement, would strut and crow most lustily.

This would bring the pious performance to a close.

John Bosco changed his program, but his reputation as the Barnum of the hamlet was secure and he knew these boys would return for more wholesome amusement. Nor was this early attractiveness confined to the young alone. John exercised it over the more mature.

Once, they tell us, on a feast day in near-by Murialdo, a public dance was being held on the village green. The church bell rang, calling the villagers to Vespers. But the whirling couples kept right on with their dance. John was known to all of them and he attempted to tell them to stop dancing and attend services. It was a nervy thing for a small boy to do, but John always had his nerve with him when God's service was at stake.

He listened in silence to rebuff after rebuff.

"Look at Holy John coming to tell us what to do!" jeered a girl.

"Hello, Kill-joy," joshed a second.

The youths were even more outspoken. "Who has appointed you to preach to us?" a young man demanded, while another told John Bosco very frankly where to go, and it wasn't into church either.

John listened patiently and then he stept to one side and began to sing a hymn to Our Lady. His boyish soprano rose above the holiday noises and music. At first, the children came around and little by little the scoffing couples. When John had gained their attention he started for the Vesper Service and we are told that this small Pied Piper led these children of an older growth into church and most effectively broke up the dance.

But with all his love for the church, it was the church's ministers who attracted him. He watched them at the altar and he learnt their sacred gestures. He was the most attentive when the priest preached. That was where he got most of his material for his little sermons, that were interlárded between his show performances. If John saw a priest on the road he would manage to come closer, hoping that he would be noticed.

Some priests are too busy to notice children and they never realize how hurt the little ones may be at this neglect. Such a priest slighted John one evening. The boy had seen the priest and had run up and politely raised his cap. The good father half acknowledged the salute and passed on. There must have been something more than an unintentional slight in the priest's manner, for John was hurt to the quick and he hastened home.

Before he got to Mama Margaret's arm he was crying bitterly.

"What is it, son?" she invited and then it came out in a flood.

Mama Margaret defended the thoughtless priest. "What would you want him to do? His mind is full of knowledge and he is thinking about God and I don't believe he would know what to say to a little boy like you."

"It would not hurt him to say a word to a child like me—only for a minute. I bet Jesus would."

Mama Margaret ignored this. It was really unanswerable. "But what would you want him to say?"

"If his mind is full of knowledge then he has studied much and he ought to know what to say to a child."

"Think, son of mine, how busy his life is. He has to prepare his sermons. He must hear confessions for long hours and then he·has all the cares of the parish . . ."

"But we children·belong to his flock, don't we?"

"Of a certainty, but he hasn't the time to waste."

"Then Jesus wasted time when He spoke to little ones and blessed them."

Mama Margaret was silenced. "My son is right. But what do you wish?"

Here John unbosomed himself: "Oh Mama, one day I want to become a priest and I will give my life to little children. They will not find me too serious or too busy, for I shall be the first to speak to them. I will call them around me and love them and make them love me. I will teach them and help them and so I will be the means of saving their souls."

These words Mama Margaret, like Mary of old, kept in her heart, pondering over them. In later years, when they were verified an hundredfold, she would retell that afternoon's confidence.

If ever a boy was marked out by God for his ministry, such a boy was John Bosco.

CHAPTER IV

THE AISLE TO THE ALTAR

GIVEN a poor boy who has made up his mind that he intends to be a priest of God some day, it is always encouraging for other boys similarly disposed to retrace the steps that determined boy took and see how the Good Shepherd will lead him unerringly around or through all difficulties and up the aisle to the altar. The little showman-preacher of Becchi was no exception.

Thank God, not all priests were like the one we met in the last chapter, who was too occupied to notice the good boy John. Over at Murialdo, the small town where John went to the market place to learn his tricks for his religious shows, was an observing priest. This was Father Calosso.

The year 1826 was a Jubilee Year and the reigning Pontiff, Leo XII, had ordered missions to be given throughout the whole countryside. One such was given near Becchi. Of course, John had a front seat at all services. This afternoon after the last service, Father Calosso was walking back to his rectory when he met a bright eleven-year-old youngster. He looked again at the lad and saw a sturdy frame, already hardened and developed by farm labor, topped by a roundish face, broad high forehead, nose and chin finely curved, dark thick curly hair. But what held his gaze was the pair of bright black eyes through which a very innocent soul gazed.

Father Calosso halted and smiled. A wonderful smile illuminated the youngster's features and he gladly fell into step with this nice priest.

"So you've been making the mission, hey, buddy?" asked Father Calosso. "Did you understand the two sermons?"

"Yes, Father," John eagerly replied and he said simply: "I understood them completely."

The priest thought this was youthful exaggeration and he decided he would call the lad's bluff. "Suppose you tell me in a few words what the preacher said."

"Well, Father, which would you like to have—the first or the second sermon?"

"You make the choice."

"The first sermon was about the need of turning to God in good time and the danger of delaying conversion. Father, if you like, I can repeat the whole of the sermon."

This was too boastful, thought Father Calosso, and he told John to repeat the sermon. John proceeded to. He gave the introduction and the three points and it took him the better part of a half hour. Father Calosso was completely convinced and what was more, he was much impressed by this child with the remarkable memory for the things of God.

The priest inquired where the lad went to school, and he learnt of the stepbrother Anthony's opposition to study and his opinion that school was a waste of time for a farmer boy and that John should work in the fields. Father Calosso pressed the boy further. "Are you anxious to go to school?"

"Yes, Father."

"Why?"

"I want to become a priest."

"Yes?"

"Father, I want to be a priest so that I can help boys to stay good. Not many priests have time for boys."

Father Calosso was much impressed with this confidence. When the two came to where their path separated he said:

"John Bosco, you keep praying to God to make you His priest and tell your good mother to come and see me next Sunday evening. Maybe something can be done about your schooling. Good-by and God bless you."

Gratefully the boy kissed the priest's hand, as the Italian custom is, and light-heartedly he ran the rest of the way home.

Mama Margaret saw Father Calosso at the appointed time, but again Anthony objected and summer became gorgeous autumn before John was able to start going to the rectory for daily lessons. Don Bosco has left us a brief reference to these early tutoring days. "I then began to learn what the spiritual life really was, for I had previously acted more like a machine, which works without knowing the reason."

Evidently the kindly Father Calosso was seeding this rich soil that was to bring forth the hundredfold and more.

But this stepbrother Anthony, now almost grown to man's estate, was one of those practical, selfish single-minded individuals. The farm must be tended at all times and he openly begrudged the hours of study that John "wasted" at Murialdo.

That winter the stepbrother's opposition came to a crisis and Mama Margaret found it necessary, in February, 1828, to send John to work on the farm of Signor Moglia. This was the twelve-year-old boy's first experience away from home.

During the summer of 1828 a priest, who was a relative of John's employer, came to the Moglia farm. He took an interest in this bright boy and during his stay, gave him a daily lesson of one hour.

John continued his work among boys, for on Sundays he tramped to near-by Moncucco where the parish priest, Father Cottino, let him instruct the boys. John repeated his shows and stories that had held spellbound the small fry of Becchi. But this farm boy was getting very little aid at his books. Then a "fairy godmother" sort of uncle sought John. This was Uncle Michael Occhiena. He found his nephew doing more farm work than study. Like our Abraham Lincoln, who at this very time was a gangling youth of nineteen, acquiring book knowledge by the light of his cabin fire, John was trying to get what little learning he could after his hard work on the farm.

Uncle Michael took his nephew back to Becchi and promised better school facilities. So after an absence of almost two years John again went daily to Father Calosso's study for lessons. But that stiff-necked stepbrother still begrudged the hours John was away from farm work. This time Father Calosso took the bright boy into his own home and tutored him. He and Mama Margaret seem to have been the first two who saw clearly that John was destined for higher things.

This steady schooling came to an abrupt halt. Father Calosso had a stroke toward the end of November, 1830. That last day the speechless priest indicated to John by signs that the contents of a money box were to be his. He gave John the key. But the heirs put in a demand and as Don Bosco has mentioned in his memoirs, "The relatives of Father Calosso came, and I gave them the key and everything." That "everything" included almost one thousand dollars that Father Calosso intended for John's further schooling.

So John at fifteen returned to his home at Becchi and that scholastic year of 1830-1831 saw the boy at Castelnuovo. Anthony, thank God, had his own farm now so there was no further opposition from that selfish quarter. The school at Castelnuovo was two and a half miles from the Bosco farm. Mama Margaret was too poor to let her boy buy a midday meal so John came home for his dinner and then returned to school for the afternoon session. Thus he had a daily hike of ten miles. No lack of exercise there, but plenty of fatigue!

A new friend appears. The tailor of Castelnuovo took an interest in the intelligent school boy from Becchi. He proposed that John live with him. So John moved into the tailor shop. He helped his kind host and between school duties learnt the tailor trade. This tailor, Signor Roberto, was also director of the choir in the parish church. He discovered that John had a good voice, so the boy became a member of the choir and learnt plain chant and sacred music.

Another change in John's school fortunes came at the end of 1831. A widow of Chieri, who was a friend of Mama Margaret, suggested that John make his home with her, while he attended the seminary school at Chieri. There was method in this widow's offer, for she wanted John's good influence to act on her son.

John moved to Chieri, attended school, picked up much knowledge of the carpenter's and iron worker's trades, and exerted his usual uplifting influence on his patroness' son and his companions.

Many a school boy will envy John Bosco some of the dreams he had at this period of his studies. For instance, one night John dreamt that his Latin master gave a certain translation to do. The boy translated the passage in his sleep. Upon awakening he wrote out his remembrance of this vivid dream and in the morning, he went to a priestly friend and had him correct the Latin and suggest certain better Italian translations.

With this corrected translation fixt in his mind, John went to school. Sure enough, the Latin master gave the identical passage. John at once wrote out his dream translation, plus the corrections, and handed the paper to his teacher. The professor was naturally surprised and delighted with the accurate translation. He listened in amazement to John's explanation. We may readily believe that his opinion of his pupil's holiness rose still higher.

There was another remarkable dream that Don Bosco summed up in this brief fashion, "At the age of sixteen I had another dream." As Pope Pius IX later commanded John to write out in detail his "dreams," which we are strongly tempted to call something nearer the supernatural, we can give this dream in fuller details.

One morning John seemed to be in high spirits. He was asked the cause and replied: "I have had splendid news. While sleeping I saw a beautiful lady. A great flock of animals were with her. She came nearer me and said: 'John, I am going to confide the whole of this flock to your care.'

" 'But how can I shepherd such numbers and where will I find the meadows to feed them?'

" 'Have no fear. I shall help you.' And with that my dream was over."

Like Joan, the shepherd maid who heard her Voices, John Bosco listened to his dreams. And those who heard the tall upstanding boy relate these "dreams" in such a matter of fact manner must have carried away with them the impression that here was a favorite of Mary. His schoolmates got into the habit of calling John "The Dreamer," but the name was bestowed with respect.

Another change of residence was coming. The widow of Chieri moved away, but the "beautiful lady" of John's dreams saw to it that another friend would show interest in this youth. So John's next host was Signor Pianta, who conducted a small restaurant in Chieri. John now was, as we would say of an American boy in similar circumstances, "working his way through college." After school hours he helped in the restaurant and the barroom. He learnt to make pastry and to mix drinks and he became a waiter and an assistant barkeeper. Signor Pianta found John most helpful and promoted him to the charge of the billiard room.

John has left us a most illuminating paragraph. Any boy "on his own," who has broken home ties and gone to work among strangers may read and reread this paragraph with profit.

Here it is in its entirety:

I had to discover the best means of dealing with my companions. I had divided them up into three classes, according to a scheme of my own; the good, the indifferent, and the bad. My plan was to avoid the last mentioned as soon as their character was discovered; with the indifferent I was on ordinary terms, treating them courteously and only having dealings with them when necessary; with the good I determined to make friends. But my familiar friends should only be among the best of them. As I was at first a complete stranger in the town I resolved not to form friendships with anyone. Several boys tried to get me to join them in their escapades, but these I usually managed to avoid by saying that my mother had entrusted me to the care of my guardian, and that I could not go with them without permission. One even suggested that I should steal money from the house in which I stayed.

John refers to his stay at the restaurant in these words:

The restaurant in which I lived for a long time was also a source of danger; for it was frequented by such a variety of persons. But the owners were good Catholics and I soon had some excellent companions.

That John was well able physically at this time to command the respect of his companions the following little incident well illustrates. One day before school hour four of John's companions "piled on" him. They bore him to the ground by their unexpected attack. Then John grabbed the arms of the top boy and pulled him down so as to squeeze the other three firmly between.

All four found themselves caught in a human vise. They struggled and twisted and squirmed in vain. John had the four caught on his back. He got to his feet and carried them in this awkward position out into the school yard. They had not bargained for this and the other school boys added "wisecracks" to their discomfort. In vain did the four promise to leave John alone if he would do likewise. John paraded them all about the yard and then returning to the classroom dumped his passengers on the floor.

His feat of strength won him new influence among his fellows, and he used it to gather a group of boys about him. These he named "The Merry Company." John was the president of this cheerful association. Wisely he knew where there was cheerfulness there was less occasion for sin.

It was while at school at Chieri that John Bosco made his first conversion. This was a young Jew named Giona, who felt attracted to John. They became friends. Then one day the Jewish boy got mixed up in some trouble. He confided his troubled conscience to John, his friend. John told him if he was a Catholic he would advise him to go to Confession and get straightened out, but that under the circumstances Confession was impossible.

"Is it?" questioned the Jewish boy. "Why can't I go and get this sin forgiven?"

It was explained tactfully to him. The upshot of this conversation was that John, at the boy's urgent request, began to teach him his catechism and his prayers. Two months later Giona was baptized and made his peace with God.

There was no question of John's vocation and fitness for the priesthood by this time. It was generally known that he was to be a priest. But to John had come a scruple, and no dream clearly to show the right way. Should he become a religious or a secular priest? It is a common difficulty to a good boy who has set his mind on higher things and it causes trouble. In truth, the roots of the difficulty lie in a lack of knowledge that the religious and the secular priesthood are two distinct vocations and the boy must seek guidance as to which of these paths God wishes him to take.

John chose this wiser plan. He sought advice in an excellent quarter. He went to Father Cafasso. He was a holy priest, stationed at the College of St. Francis of Assisi in Turin, and he is now a Saint. Father Cafasso listened to the boy, told him he would pray over the matter and later advised John Bosco to continue at the Seminary and prepare for the work God had planned for him—that of a secular priest.

Mama Margaret, when she learned of her son's indecision paid him a special visit and said: "John, I only desire that you think over carefully what your right vocation is and then follow it. The parish priest tells me I should advise you not to become a religious, but a secular priest, so that you will be in a position to aid me. But in the question of my child's vocation, I am not to be considered. Remember that God must come first. I was born poor and have lived so and I wish to die poor. If when you became a secular priest you had the misfortune to become rich, I should not even come to see you. Now you understand my position."

There is the valiant woman of the Scriptures speaking out her heart's sentiments. No wonder such a mother had such a son! John Bosco would have found it hard to be otherwise than a zealous priest.

So John continued his preparatory studies. On October 25, 1835, he was invested with the clerical cassock. And five days later his actual theological studies began at the Seminary of Chieri.

Here should be inserted the resolutions that the young Seminarian drew up for his guidance:

(1) the boyish shows he had put on to attract children should be abandoned, as not becoming.

(2) retirement and temperance should be practiced daily.

(3) his reading should be along religious lines only.

(4) the slightest occasion against purity should be avoided.

(5) meditation and spiritual reading should be added to his daily pious practices.

(6) every day he resolved to speak on some edifying example to his companions.

These youthful resolutions show clearer than many paragraphs of explanation that the spiritual side of this holy boy was well developed. And what is more, it is a matter of record that these resolutions were not the usual New Year's ones that are forgotten long before the coming of February. John put them into practice and his companions of the Seminary days have testified that he kept them, whole and entire.

On Lætare Sunday, 1840, which fell on March 29 that year, John Bosco received the tonsure and the four Minor Orders. On the following September 18 he became a Subdeacon. March 27, 1841, he was raised to the Diaconate and the Desired Day came on the Saturday after Pentecost, June 5, 1841, when the Bishop of Turin, Archbishop Fransoni, ordained John Bosco a priest of God forever. Then for the first time he was called by the Italian title for Father, the title by which the world knows him—Don Bosco.

His memoirs tell graphically of the next memorable days:

I celebrated my First Mass in the Church of St. Francis of Assisi, where Father Cafasso, my director and particular benefactor, was.

The people of my native place were most anxious for me to go home, as it was many years since a First Mass had been celebrated there, but I preferred to say it in Turin away from all distractions. It was said at the Altar of the Guardian Angel, on the Gospel side of the Church. . . . At the Memento, in that ever-memorable Mass I took care to mention particularly all my masters in the Seminary, and my spiritual and temporal benefactors, and especially the lamented Father Calosso, to whom I always regarded myself as much indebted. It is a pious belief that the favors asked by a priest at his First Mass are invariably granted; I asked in a special manner for the gift of *Efficacy in Word*, in order to do good to souls.

Whether Don Bosco received the other favors he petitioned for in that First Mass, we do not know, but that he received "efficacy in word" there is not the slightest doubt. But the people who had known and loved John as a boy were not to be disappointed. His memoirs enlighten us:

On Thursday, the Feast of Corpus Christi, I satisfied the desire of the people of my native place. I went to Castelnuovo where I sang the Mass and carried the Blessed Sacrament in the Procession. The Rector insisted on inviting a goodly number to the repast and all were extremely pleased, for I was somehow much beloved by the people there, and all rejoiced in what concerned my welfare and advancement. That evening I spent at home. But when I was near the place, and saw where I had had my first dream, at the age of nine, I could not restrain my emotion and exclaimed: "How wonderful are the designs of Divine Providence! God has indeed raised up a lowly child, to place him among the chiefs of the people."

That evening at home around the old familiar table Mama Margaret said to Father John: "My son, you are now a priest and you will offer the Holy Sacrifice; you are therefore nearer to Jesus Christ. But remember that to commence your priestly life means that you will begin to suffer. You may not perceive it at once, but after a time the truth of my words will be clear to you. I am sure that you will pray for me, whether I am alive or dead; that is enough for me. Henceforth devote yourself entirely to the salvation of souls."

In these words the illiterate Mama Margaret has summed up the reward she, the mother of a priest, asked for herself and the real life work that was opening before her anointed son. That joyous evening those two must have gone over the steps and the difficulties and the helps that had stopt and had advanced the long journey of the boy from the poor farm at Becchi to the altar of God. The words of the Dream Mother now sounded clearer. "Make yourself humble, determined and strong."

John Bosco had come safely up the aisle to the altar and now as Father John he was equipped to begin the changing of those animals of his dream into lambs—a work that he would continue till his death, forty-seven years later.

CHAPTER V

A WANDERING ORATORY

To young Father John Bosco came the offer of three possible assignments. He could have been a tutor to the sons of a nobleman in Genoa. But Mama Margaret, when she heard of the offer exclaimed: "My son in the houses of the wealthy! . . . What would the salary avail me or his brothers, if it hurt his soul!" She knew her son's heart well enough to know he would never accept such a comfortable living.

The other two assignments were, either to be parish priest at Murialdo, or assistant at Castelnuovo. Father John wisely decided to consult his old Confessor and so he walked to Turin. Father Cafasso's advice was to enter the St. Francis of Sales Institute for Higher Theological Studies. Don Bosco accepted this as the Will of God and on November 3, 1841, at this House for the Clergy at Turin, he commenced his further courses in moral theology and sacred eloquence.

It was in these days that Don Bosco met a saintly Turin priest; now Saint Joseph Benedict Cottolengo. The latter stopt the zealous young priest and plucking his coat, made this prediction: "Don Bosco, your coat is too thin. Better get one of stronger material for the days will come when it will be pulled about by many boys."

Looking over the background of John's boyhood it was obvious that boy work was to be his special vocation.

He himself has penned his ideal along these lines, when he wrote shortly after his ordination:

> The young, who form the most cherished and most attractive portion of human society, and in whom are centered all our hopes for a happy future, are by no means intrinsically perverse or inclined to wickedness. Once you have counteracted the carelessness of some parents, the effects of idleness, and of evil companions, it becomes the easiest thing imaginable to instil into their young hearts the principles of order, of good behavior, of respect toward others, and to accustom them to the practice of religion; and if you should meet any who are already spoiled at that tender age, it is the result of neglect rather than of downright wickedness. These are the ones who especially need a helping hand; the difficulty lies in finding the means of gathering them together in order to speak to them and control them. This was the mission the Son of God took upon himself; this can be done by His Holy Religion alone, which is eternal and unchangeable in itself; which was and always will be the teacher of mankind; which contains a doctrine so perfect that it is suited to all times, and adapted to the different characters of all men. Among the means suitable for the diffusion of the spirit of religion among the untaught and ill-disposed will be found the Oratories.

It is not hard to imagine that a young, zealous, holy priest, loving boys because they are boys, would have to wait long to put those sentiments into practice. The Dream Mother arranged things that the start of the famous Don Bosco Oratories—or Boys' Clubs as we should call them—would come on the Feast of Her Immaculate Conception. It was December 8, 1841, and Don Bosco was vested in the sacristy of the Church of St. Francis of Assisi and waiting for an altar boy who had taken a late sleep.

The young priest's preparatory prayers were violently interrupted. He turned around and saw the sacristan attempting to force a strange boy to serve his Mass.

Don Bosco heard the lad say: "How can I, I don't know. Let go of me!"

The sacristan gave the lad a cuff on the ear and ordered him out of the sacristy. Here the priest, who had seen enough, told the angry sacristan to quit it. He beckoned to the strange boy and the youngster, sensing a champion, came at once. Don Bosco whispered to him not to mind the sacristan, but to come back after Mass as he wished to speak with him.

When Don Bosco had finished his Thanksgiving, there was the lad standing quietly in the corner of the sacristy.

"What's your name, buddy?"

"Bartholomew Garelli."

"Live here in Turin?"

"No, Father, I come from Asti."

"Parents living?"

"No, I'm an orphan."

"You're about fifteen, aren't you?"

"Yes."

"Can you read and write?"

"No."

"Do you know your prayers?"

"No."

"Have you made your First Holy Communion?"

"No."

"Do you attend Sunday School?"

"No; I am too old and the little kids would make fun of me."

Here was evidently a neglected one and the heart of Don Bosco warmed to him. "Suppose, buddy, I were to offer to teach you alone, would you come and learn your catechism?"

The boy smiled and agreed: "Surely, but . . ." he added the condition from sad experience with adults, "that is, if you promise not to beat me."

"You needn't fear. When do we begin—this evening?"

"Suits me, Father. Right now if you say so."

Don Bosco was agreeable and seating Bartholomew alongside him there in the sacristy, he taught him how to bless himself and then the answer to the old, old question, "Who made you?"

Bartholomew Garelli was invited to return the following Sunday and bring some of his companions. During the week he must have talked about the novelty of having some adult speak kindly to him, for he returned on the next Sunday with six other "devils," all more ignorant of the things of God than himself.

Don Bosco met the gang and led them into a small room opening off the sacristy. In this room was a vine growing up through a hole in the floor and spreading all over the roof. Don Bosco did not know at the time how symbolic that vine was of the work he was seeding at that very moment; a work destined to spread and spread. For he was starting his first Oratory with those seven boys. Very elementary was the instruction that he gave those poor neglected Turin boys. He had to start at the "basement" of the catechism. But these boys and more who came on succeeding Sundays to that room of the spreading vine, were quick to sense that in this young priest they had met one who was kindly and understanding.

If you have ever had the opportunity of listening to boys off their guard discussing their superiors, you will have noticed how shrewdly they size up the pretences and short-comings of these same men and women. But just as readily they penetrate into the wholesomeness and whole-heartedness of those who know boys. Such a one was young Don Bosco. Without sacrificing any of his priestly dignity he stoopt to enter the boys' world. He knew and enjoyed their games. Their big interests became his. And he won the hearts of boys if ever a boy's man did.

Here one is tempted to wish Scoutcraft had been in existence when Don Bosco began his Oratories. What an instrument for God's work he would have made of that boy program! Those who are familiar with cheerful Boy Scouts, their Oath and their Laws; those who have camped with these eager khaki-clad youngsters and have listened in on the happy weekly meeting nights, will be struck with the similarity of Don Bosco's efforts to reach the neglected future citizens of Turin and the problems that a successful Catholic Scoutmaster has in the less wealthy sections of any American city. All unconsciously Don Bosco was a Scoutmaster without a peer.

What time he had from his higher ecclesiastical studies at the Institute of St. Francis of Assisi, he devoted to the ever-increasing troops of boys who sought him out. Don Bosco called his work the Oratory of St. Francis of Sales. He had always had great devotion to the gentle Bishop of Geneva, so he made him patron of this good work and he practiced his gentleness in all his dealings with his "rogues." For now Don Bosco began to call himself the Chief of the Rogues.

All decent people like boys, but some prefer them asleep or at play three blocks away. Unfortunately, these young-sters who habitually dressed as Jackie Coogan was accus-tomed to in his pictures, a few years ago, were noisy and given to settling their sudden disputes there and then. So the budding Oratory was heading into, what sailors aptly call, "a spell of dirty weather." Don Bosco's Sun-day classes were tolerated while he was pursuing his higher studies at St. Francis of Assisi. Everybody recog-nized that he was doing a wholesome work among the poorer boys of the big city, but again they did not want the noisy crowds near-by.

Then in 1844 Don Bosco finished his advanced studies at the Institute attached to St. Francis and a move became imperative. He was eager to remain in Turin and when the chaplaincy of St. Philomena's Hospice was offered to him, gladly he accepted. He had one doubt. Would his boys follow him to his new residence? The next Sunday settled that question beyond any shadow of a doubt. They would and did and brought more to receive instructions.

But a new difficulty arose. There was no chapel attached to the Hospice and where would these boys hear Mass? Don Bosco, always resourceful, settled this prob-lem by taking his ragged regiment to various churches in near-by parts of the city. We can almost see the respect-able part of the congregation shifting their valuables to a safer pocket when Don Bosco's gang came in to hear Mass.

The Marchioness Barolo, who was the Foundress of St. Philomena's Hospice, showed her interest in the chaplain's extra work. She permitted him to have two small rooms. These he adapted to his purposes and made one of them a chapel. Again on December 8—this time in the year 1844—he dedicated these rooms, calling them the Oratory of St. Francis of Sales. It was just three years since he had started his boy work with young Bartholomew Garelli and this date, December 8, 1841, was afterward considered the start of the Salesian Oratories. Another priest had now been attracted to Don Bosco and his boy work. This was Father Borel. Between the two of them the shifting crowds of homeless and friendless waifs of the sidewalks of Turin found friends and teachers.

To the elementary Catechetical instructions Don Bosco and his companion now added evening classes, in which they taught some of the boys to read and write. These were the first evening classes to be conducted in Italy.

Everything went along for a few months at the Hospice of St. Philomena till the Foundress, Marchioness Barolo, who evidently still had a firm hand on the management, decided the coming of the boys at night and on Sundays was too much for the Hospice's quietness. The Marchioness told Don Bosco, politely but emphatically, that he was either to devote all his time to his chaplaincy and send the boys about their thieving business, or seek other quarters.

Sadly Don Bosco broke the news of this expulsion to his ragged friends. He told them next Sunday he would meet them and conduct them to the Church of the Cemetery of St. Peter in Chains. But here one Sunday was enough for the priest's housekeeper. She stormed at the noise of the playing boys, threatened to call the police, and influenced the priest to lodge a complaint against the thieving, loud, etc., ragamuffins, who infested the sanctity of the holy place, etc., etc.

Turning on gentle Don Bosco she raged: "By next Sunday, at whatever cost, I shall not be disturbed by you and these brats." Don Bosco looked at the angry housekeeper and then told the boys who surrounded him: "Poor woman, she is right. By next Sunday she will not be here to see us. Come on, boys."

They followed him and during the week they learnt that the woman had died suddenly.

During that same week Don Bosco arranged with the Municipal authorities to use the Church of St. Martin near the Dora. And to this new locality the wandering Oratory headed.

It was at this period that Don Bosco made his famous "transplanted cabbages" sermon. He said:

"You know, my dear boys, that cabbages do not become full and large, unless they are transplanted, and this applies to our Oratory. Up till now it has been moved from place to place, and in every one of them, it has increased remarkably. The time spent at the Hospice was not without good fruit, and there, as at St. Francis of Assisi, you had spiritual and temporal assistance, improvement of both body and soul, catechism and instruction, games and sports. At the Hospice a beginning was made of a real Oratory; there we had a chapel to ourselves, in a suitable and retired place; but Divine Providence has disposed that we should leave it and be transplanted here. Shall we be here long? We do not know! But whatever happens, we hope that like the transplanted cabbages, our Oratory will increase in the number of boys devoted to the practice of virtue, improving in their knowledge of music and other subjects, and that we shall have in time not only Sunday and evening classes, but day schools as well. So do not let us be downhearted. Let us put all our trust in God, and He will take care of us."

In this recorded sermon of Don Bosco we have a fairly

accurate picture of the activities and the vicissitudes of the shifting Oratory.

This "assemblage of vagabonds," as some of the peace-loving folks called Don Bosco's noisy three hundred, now moved on and invaded St. Martin's. There was an unfenced field near-by and this was converted into a play-ground, for Don Bosco always was a strong believer in mixing religion with healthy doses of recreation. Here the Oratory began an uncertain existence.

Sometimes Don Bosco varied the Sunday program. He would tell his boys to meet at his lodgings. One of these wandering boys has given us this account of these religious hikes.

At the end of each meeting, before separating, the good Father always told us the excursion for next Sunday; the road, program, and hour; gave advice as to our conduct, and asked us to be as numerous as possible—"If you have any comrades, invite them from me, the more the merrier." The walk for the next Sunday was a topic of conversation during the week in our workshops and families; it exacted more attention, obedience, and application to duty, so as not to incur the punishment of being kept at home. The chief walks, carefully varied, were; to the Mount of the Capuchins, to Our Lady of the Fields, to Pozzo di Strada; and to Our Lady of the Lakes at Avigliana. These happy days are engraved in our memories; piety and joy reigned among us, and influenced our future lives. Arrived at some church in the precincts of a town, Don Bosco asked leave to celebrate Mass. The permission was always granted and then at a signal, the noisy band gathered together to attend with a celerity and unanimity which amazed the bystanders. Catechism followed, then breakfast: the grass or the rocks supplied the place of tables, forks were unnecessary; as for wine, the rivulets or fountains freely supplied what was needful; those who had too much shared with less fortunate boys and Don Bosco fed those who had none. It is true, bread failed now and then; but gaiety and a good appetite never. Continuing our walk, we stopped somewhere to chant Vespers, the itinerant Oratory already possessed a good choir; Catechism was heard a second time; the Rosary was recited while walking; and at sunset we marched again into Turin, fatigued, but with light consciences and contented hearts.

The winter of 1845-1846 was approaching and these Sunday hikes must of a necessity be abandoned. So Don Bosco rented some rooms of a Signor Moretta. Here his street boys met and instruction classes were held. But the drawback to this arrangement was there was no chapel. Don Bosco took the boys to the neighboring Church of the Consolata.

With the coming of spring and an increase in the number òf boys, the long-suffering neighbors protested to Don Bosco and the police. Again the Oratory was on the march. It stopt at a field for a few Sundays but the owner took a rueful look at his field and once more priest and boys were looking for a meeting place.

The storm of opposition to Don Bosco's boy work now broke with sharp violence. So many complaints were coming to the Municipal authorities that the Marquis di Cavour, the Mayor of Turin, sent for Don Bosco and told him quite frankly that he and his hoodlums were disturbing the peace and he was to discontinue his Sunday riots. Don Bosco argued that his assemblies were rather a help to maintaining public order. Wasn't he teaching these lawless boys law and order and respect for legitimate authority? Besides, what he was doing was with the full knowledge and approval of the Archbishop of Turin. The interview ended without any results. The Mayor learnt that King Charles Albert looked with favor on Don Bosco's work. His Majesty had even contributed some money to further the Oratory. Cavour, a prudent politician, promptly changed his attitude.

But among the local clergy the opposition was rising. They looked on this free-lance Sunday School as an encroachment on their parochial rights. Some of these objectors made the remarkable argument to the Archbishop that there were as many catechetical teachers in Don Bosco's Oratory as there were in all the churches of Turin! For Don Bosco now has some boy-loving young priests and seminarians helping him. If the clerical complaint was true, it did not sound well for the religious instruction that was being given the young of Turin at that date. These objectors asked the questions: "Is it not the place for the various parish priests to prepare the children for the reception of First Confession and First Communion?" "How will we know who has made his Easter duty and who has not?" "Wouldn't it be better to transfer Don Bosco to some country parish where he would be unable to disturb the city parishes?"

The Archbishop, Monsignor Fransoni, listened and then sending for Don Bosco asked him how he answered these objections. Don Bosco readily showed that the majority of his boys were orphans or the children of Savoyards, Lombards, Swiss, not the sons of Turin parents. As for his Turin boys, they were street urchins and attended no church. If His Grace ordered the Oratory discontinued would these boys go to the various parish churches, or would they go back to the streets and pick up their religious education there?

The upshot of the interview was the Archbishop again gave his approval to the boy work and he told the objecting clergy that they might with profit go and do likewise. So the wandering Oratory had a short respite, but Signor Moretta canceled Don Bosco's lease of the three rooms and again a new meeting place had to be procured.

This time Don Bosco and his boys met in an open field. Father Borel, who had followed Don Bosco most faithfully in his wanderings, was beginning to lose hope of the success of the enterprise.

"Give it up," was the burden of his conversation.

"No; God has begun this work, and He must complete it. Good has been done these boys that we have gathered at considerable difficulty."

"But we can't continue to hold meetings in a field! What if it rains next Sunday?"

Don Bosco smiled. "Soon we'll hold them in the new Oratory."

"Where is it?" the more practical-minded Father Borel wanted to know.

"I see it already built. I see the Church, a house, and playgrounds. I see the whole Oratory."

"And I see a rough field with plenty of weeds and dirt."

"I cannot yet say where, but they do exist and they are for our work."

Father Borel thought pityingly, "Poor Don Bosco, this hard work has had its effect! His mind is going fast!"

What Don Bosco has not revealed was that he had had

another of his remarkable dreams. He had spoken of it
to his Confessor, Father Cafasso, and that saintly man had
reassured Don Bosco that he might trust this dream.
But Father Borel's fears were carried to others, who were
only too anxious to believe them true.

There is recorded a conversation that Don Bosco had
with some of these over-zealous clerical friends. It reveals
the gentle humor that was ever characteristic of him. One
afternoon several of these priests accosted him.

"You should not act so mulishly in this matter,
Father John. It is clear that Divine Providence dis-
approves of your boy work. Don't go against Providence! Of course, it would be a sacrifice to your
tender heart to send these young ragamuffins about
their business, but you must do it. Think of the
good you can do in parish work."

Don Bosco replied: "My friends, you speak of
Divine Providence, but in a mistaken manner. I am
by no means unable to carry on this Oratory work.
Providence has sent me these boys and I shall not
send even one of them away. Rest assured of that.
Wait, I am perfectly satisfied that God will provide
in His own good time all things necessary. . . . The
means are at hand . . . and if they will not let me
hire a place, I shall build one, with the help of Our
Blessed Mother. We shall have great buildings,
capable of holding all the boys who care to come; we
shall have workshops of every kind in which the boys
may learn a trade. There will be a fine playground
and portico, a magnificent church, heads of trades,
masters, and priests who will have special care of
those who have a vocation."

Don Bosco stopped painting his rosy picture when he saw the pitying looks that his two listeners were exchanging. Their worst fears were realized. Mad as a March hare!

They would see how far this insanity had gone.

"Then you intend to found a new Order?" one asked.

"And what if I had such an idea?" Don Bosco parried.

But his questioner persisted: "What will be the habit of your religious?"

"Virtue," Don Bosco told him.

"Very good, but something more will be necessary, otherwise the police will interfere."

"Then I should wish them to have a sort of overall with sleeves like the workmen."

This was good. They all laughed heartily.

When they were exhausted, Don Bosco objected:

"Does this strike you as being funny or strange? But you must surely know that such a garb would represent poverty and that a religious order cannot last without being true to the spirit of poverty."

"We understand perfectly," Don Bosco's self-invited Board of Faith and Morals rose to depart.

Quickly the rumor spread throughout clerical circles in Turin that poor Don Bosco had gone quite out of his head from the hardships and hard work that those dirty street vagabonds had caused him. Wasn't it a pity! But, stubborn man, he never would listen to those who knew better, etc., etc.

Even the Archiepiscopal Curia listened to these rumors and sent a private examiner. We do not know what Don Bosco's sense of humor led him to tell this priest, but his report was the same as the two former examiners. The Vicar General of the Archdiocese, Father Ravina, knew the worth of this priest devoted to boy work, and saw through the designs of those who were spreading the insanity rumors. He refused to permit any action.

But the Clan of Our Brothers' Keepers decided to take matters in their own hands. Two clan members in good standing went to an insane asylum, explained the sad case of a young priest who had broken down mentally from overwork. They arranged that on the next afternoon he was to be brought quietly to the asylum in a closed carriage. The Superintendent understood perfectly. He would see that the unfortunate occupant of the closed carriage was given rest and retirement.

With all arrangements made to their satisfaction the reverend two drove up to Don Bosco's humble rooms. They got Don Bosco into a discussion on the great future of his Oratory. It was quite clear to them that the disease had made progress in the past few days. Madder than a March hare was he.

Don Bosco had been watching his visitors and he fathomed their designs. But he kept his own counsel. Rather, we can imagine he smiled quietly and dropt a few harmless remarks that were promptly misinterpreted.

So when the two suggested that he come for a drive this lovely afternoon, he accepted their kind invitation. At the open door of the carriage, the visitors steps courteously aside to permit Don Bosco to enter.

"Your ecclesiastical dignity will not permit me to enter first," demurred Don Bosco.

That was true, so the two stept into the carriage. Quickly Don Bosco fastened close the door and told the driver to whip up his horse. Those were just the instructions that the driver had received from the two and he did so. He drove at a gallop to the asylum, not listening to the angry cries that came from the closed carriage.

The asylum gates were open, as per arrangement, and the steaming horse and carriage were driven rapidly up the drive.

The Superintendent had his attendants also instructed, and though they were rather surprised to see two clerical gentlemen in the closed carriage, when they had been told to expect one, nevertheless they took them gently but forcibly toward the appointed rooms. There was no doubt but that they were mad.

The two priests were furious at the way they had fallen into their own trap. They protested that they were perfectly sane, there had been a horrible mistake. The attendants were used to such explanations. Nearly all the patients used them on their arrival.

"Call the Superintendent. He will identify us."

"Sorry, but he is off the grounds at present."

"Then call the chaplain. He knows we are sane."

"Sorry again. The chaplain is at dinner and you understand he can't be disturbed."

"I tell you I'm not insane."

Despite their flood of protests the two were led to their rooms and left there safely behind locked doors.

Eventually, the chaplain, possibly taking pity on poor Don Bosco, came to the rooms. His surprise equaled the relief of the imprisoned two. Quickly their sanity and identity were established and they quit the asylum. They had learned their lesson. Don Bosco had method in his madness. And afterwards they left him severely alone. But the story was too good to keep and it lost nothing in the telling. It did check the enthusiasm of those who thought Don Bosco insane.

Shortly after the asylum incident, Don Bosco saw the two priests on the street. But they saw him, too, and they turned down a side street, not caring to face him.

So the Oratory continued in the field near the Church of Our Lady of the Field. Then the lease ran out. Don Bosco was alone. From a worldly standpoint, the future looked black and threatening for the Oratory. That last Sunday Don Bosco told his boys that he did not know where they were to meet on the following Sunday. He told them they were like fledglings whose nest had been destroyed. He begged them to redouble their prayers and, like himself, not to lose hope. He knew Our Lady too well for that.

It was in truth the darkness before the dawn, for the wandering Oratory was, within a few hours, to come within sight of its permanent location.

CHAPTER VI

A DREAM COMES TRUE

INDEED, it was the darkness before the dawn—in the fortunes of Don Bosco's itinerant Oratory. That Palm Sunday of 1846 he had told the boys either their prayer would be heard or they must disband. When boys want anything and want it with a will, they can pray. "The assemblage of vagabonds" stormed Heaven that morning at Our Lady of the Fields. Later, Don Bosco led them to the field and he conducted catechetical classes and directed their recreation.

Then it happened. One Pancrace Soave came into the noisy field and asked where the priest in charge was. Several willing boys pointed out their priestly friend, who had gone apart to pray. Soave sought Don Bosco and said: "Father, I hear you seek a laboratory?"

"Not a laboratory, but an Oratory is what I need badly."

"It is all the same to me. I know just the place you want, in the Valdocco section of the town, but it is not rent free."

"I'll pay rent, if it is just the place I want."

"Then come with me and I'll show it to you."

Don Bosco followed this self-appointed real-estate agent and he was led to another field that had a large shed erected in the middle of it. It was in the last stages of neglect. The roof leaked and the walls let in ample daylight. Don Bosco shook his head. This would never do for his purposes.

But Pancrace Soave was interested in renting his friend's land. He insisted that Don Bosco come with him and have a talk with the owner, Signor Pinardi. Together the three returned to inspect the shed. Don Bosco found more difficulties. The dilapidated structure was erected over the side of a hill and the uphill side was only three feet high.

"This will never do!" exclaimed Don Bosco. "Why, my smaller boys could hardly stand erect inside this shed. And as for the larger ones and myself . . ."

"Listen, Father," said Pinardi, "you want a laboratory. I'll dig out the earth inside so that all of your boys can stand erect and then you'll have your laboratory."

Again Don Bosco explained that it was an "Oratory" he desired.

"Good. Oratory then," agreed Pinardi. "You rent the shed and turn it into a chapel, I'll give a silver lamp and my wife and I'll take two seats in it."

"What is the rent?" asked Don Bosco.

"It is nothing. I'll let you have it for sixty dollars."

Don Bosco was beginning to see the possibilities of this shed and he said: "You are right. That is low rental. I'll give you sixty-four dollars, but on one condition."

"What is that?"

"That you make me out a lease and agree to have two feet of that floor in the shed hollowed out before next Sunday."

"O. K.," readily agreed Signor Pinardi.

With joy in his heart Don Bosco sought his homeless boys and a great shout of delight went up from the gang when their spiritual father announced: "My boys, we do not have to disband. Our Lady has given us a home. Let us kneel down and recite a decade of the rosary in thanksgiving." Rarely were more fervent Hail Marys said.

Though the boys did not yet know it, this shed of Pinardi's about fifty feet long by eighteen feet wide, was to be the first building of the future Oratory of St. Francis of Sales.

During Holy Week Pinardi and his helper, Pancrace Soave, with the aid of some of Don Bosco's older boys, made the dirt fly. The flooring was lowered. The walls were repaired, the roof was made almost rainproof.

So great progress was made by willing hands that with the dawn of Easter, April 12, 1846, the shed was ready for the boys. Don Bosco said Mass, gave Holy Communion, and continued his Sunday School work. Father Borel, and other priests assisted him and he had need of them, for the boys now numbered almost five hundred.

The gathering of such a crowd of street boys could not escape notice. Many people came to criticize and remained to praise. It was known now that the Archbishop had given Don Bosco the faculties to act as a parish priest to these street urchins who came to the shed-chapel. He had episcopal sanction to say Mass, preach, hear Confessions, and give Holy Communion.

The records of those first permanent days read as though many citizens of Turin, clerical and lay, made a rush to get on the "bandwagon." The "poor Don Bosco," who had been thought a little weak in his mind, now was spoken of as the zealous boy worker. The tide had changed. Basking in the sunshine of his self-appointed critics had no more effect on honest Don Bosco than had their previous strictures on his labors.

Soon a smaller near-by shed was leased. This was a wet-weather shelter when the field could not be used for recreation. Don Bosco had been quietly selecting some of the more intelligent boys, instructing them in his successful methods, and appointing them as assistant teachers. The plan worked. He had now teachers to help him.

With his Sunday School sheltered, Don Bosco hired some rooms near-by. In these he restarted his evening classes in the three R's, in Italian, French, geography and history. His youthful teachers were a great aid; possibly, most of their inspiration came from the contagious enthusiasm of their beloved director.

The Oratory of St. Francis of Sales was in full swing, but the strain of those pioneer days was too much for even the iron constitution of its Founder. The doctor diagnosed his sickness as inflammation of the lungs. Don Bosco was forced to stay in bed. Mama Margaret tramped in from Becchi and became his nurse. Father Borel took over the direction of the new Oratory, and Don Bosco's boys made the hospital, where their Benefactor lay deadly ill, a place of pilgrimage. Openly these tearful-faced boys knelt in the street and offered up fervent prayers for his recovery.

A week after he was taken down, the Last Sacraments were administered. The doctor said he was going to die. Father Borel thought that the one who could most effectively pray for Don Bosco's recovery was none other than Don Bosco himself. So he came to the bedside and said: "Father John, ask God to cure you. Many need you. You ask Him and He will hear you."

But Don Bosco replied: "May God's Holy Will be done!"

"That is not sufficient. You make that prayer more specific. Ask God for your recovery for the sake of these five hundred little beggars who are crowding about the altar of Our Lady of Consolation and are blocking up the street outside. Why, some of these monkeys are making vows of penance for your recovery that would task the strength of the monks of the desert!"

Don Bosco listened and his eyes filled. The appeal to the faith and love of his boys won him over. He consented to pray, "God, please cure me, if it is Your Holy Will."

Father Borel breathed a sigh of relief. "Now I know you will be out of that bed shortly." And he went to broadcast the news that Don Bosco was at length praying for his own recovery. The assistant's faith in the efficacy of Don Bosco's prayers was rewarded. The very next day Don Bosco was reported convalescing.

That illness publicly demonstrated the affection—rather, the passionate love, that the street boys of Turin had for their Best Friend.

But the real demonstration came when Don Bosco made his first public appearance after his illness. It was a Sunday and the boys were waiting outside the hospital to escort the invalid to the Oratory. Don Bosco had a cane to help him walk. He did not use that cane, for some of the bigger boys grabbed up a chair. Don Bosco was seated in it, much against his will, and it was hoisted to the shoulders of the bearers. Thus, with Don Bosco impersonating the Holy Father on a makeshift Sedia Gestatoria, the parade started. Other boys ran ahead. They were not silent. They threw flowers along the entire road from the hospital to the Oratory at Valdocco.

Once the converted shed was reached a *Te Deum* was

intoned that was heard a quarter of a mile away. Don
Bosco spoke briefly to his boys. "My dear friends, God
should be the object of your love. He gave me the means
to do anything that I have done. He has restored my
health, I am His to serve; yours, to serve for His sake.
For Him and for you I wish to employ my life."

There was no question of Don Bosco's resuming the
full round of his duties just yet. The doctor recommended
that he go home to Becchi with Mama Margaret and, in
his native air, get back his strength. Obediently he set out
with his mother. Father Borel aided by several young
priests, Father Vola and Father Pacchiotti, took over the
Oratory work during his absence.

At Becchi Don Bosco was received with open arms. He
met his brother Joseph's children and in the company of
these nieces and nephews, he grew slowly stronger.

It was of this time that several anecdotes are told
which shed much light on Don Bosco's character and
influence.

Don Bosco had been for a stroll through the woods and
suddenly a man stept out from behind the bole of a tree
and brandishing an evil-looking knife, demanded in con-
ventional highway man style "Your money or your life!"

Don Bosco must have smiled at the first demand. He
looked sharply at the would-be robber and in that glance
placed him. Motioning to the man to put down that knife,
he said. "My friend, neither the one nor the other. And is
it you indeed who would wish to harm Don Bosco?"

Hearing this name the robber dropt his knife and his
eyes. He had recognized the young priest who had shown
him kindness, when he was serving a sentence in a Turin
prison. The motive for the attempted robbery came out
in the subsequent conversation. This man, released from

prison and rejected by his family, had found it hard to get work and had drifted back into former easier ways.

Don Bosco suggested Confession and the humbled man made it there and then in the woods. When he got up from his knees, Don Bosco said: "Come along with me. I know where you will receive supper and lodging."

He led the man to his own home. Mrs. Bosco, growing anxious at her son's prolonged absence, was standing at the gate.

"Mama Margaret, here is a friend of mine. We met in the woods and I have persuaded him to have supper and spend the night with us."

Both Mama Margaret and Joseph Bosco suspected what kind of a friend this was, and they adopted a policy of watchful waiting that evening and night. In the morning the guest went to Mass and later he left with a letter of recommendation from Don Bosco that soon put him on his feet.

The other anecdote that shows what an influence Don Bosco was exerting in the Confessional occurred at this time. Among Don Bosco's many extra Oratory duties was that of Confessor to a Boys' School, conducted by the Christian Brothers in Turin. When Confession day came around and Don Bosco did not come to hear the lads' confessions they determined to go to him. It was late in the morning when some two hundred youthful penitents hiked into Becchi in search of their beloved Father Confessor.

Don Bosco received them kindly, led them to the church, heard their confessions, and then with the aid of Mama Margaret, his brother Joseph, and some boy-loving neighbors a hasty lunch was made up for the shriven boys and they were packed off on their return hike to Turin.

Convalescence was rapid in the bracing country air of his native place and by August Don Bosco's strength was restored enough for him to plan to return to his neglected Oratory. Reports had reached him that he was missed there. Those who substituted for him lacked his knack of dealing with noisy boys and affairs there were drifting into a dangerous state. There were more than domestic difficulties connected with the Oratory of St. Francis of Sales.

Don Bosco's permission to live at the Hospice had been withdrawn. Rather, he had been given the alternative of being Chaplain there and cutting adrift from his beloved boy work, or being Pastor to his street urchins and severing his connection with the Hospice. It is easy to guess the decision that Don Bosco came to. He would leave the Hospice rooms.

Then the problem presented itself. If he lived at the Oratory, who would keep his household? In his perplexity Don Bosco went to visit his friend the pastor at near-by Castelnuovo. The priest listened to him and then proposed: "You have a mother who is kindly and inspires respect. She is strong enough to be your housekeeper. Take her back to Turin with you."

John Bosco walked back to the Becchi farm with this plan in his mind. He proposed it that evening in the old family house.

Mama Margaret listened quietly to her son's proposal. Then she prayed for a few minutes and looking up with a smile said simply: "Johnnie, that is not a bad idea. Joseph and my grandchildren here do not need me. You have been sick and do. So I shall pack my bundle when you do."

Her son Joseph put up vigorous objections to his

mother's intended departure for the Valdocco section of
Turin. That section did not have a good reputation.
Some of the neighbors and old friends of the Widow
Bosco added other objections, but to all of them she
replied, "I believe it is the will of God that I should go
and help John with his boys."

It was on November 3, 1846, that Don Bosco and Mama
Margaret started to walk the thirty miles from Becchi to
Turin. They traveled light. He carried his Breviary, a
Missal, and some books; she had in a basket some linen
and her clothes. Thus equipped, as the Apostles of old,
the mother and son hiked along the dusty roads. A Turin
priest, Father Vola, who met them en route, stopt and
questioned the two. He learnt they had no money; there
were no preparations at the end of the journey to receive
them. Touched at this poverty Father Vola reached into
his pockets. He had no money with him either. So he
unfastened his watch and gave it to Don Bosco, telling
him to sell it and use the proceeds for his rascals. Don
Bosco accepted the alms, saying, "See, Mama Margaret,
Providence is coming to our needs very quickly!"

So Don Bosco and Mama Margaret came to the converted shed at Valdocco. There, for the remaining eight
years of her life, Mama Margaret was housekeeper and
mother in general to all the street boys who sought and
received the hospitality of the Oratory of St. Francis of
Sales.

Very quickly Mama Margaret set to rights the poor
furnishings of her son's room and installed herself in
another. Her days were filled with the boys who came
crowding around. Her motherly heart opened and took
them all in to give a mother's care to so many who had
never known it before. For Don Bosco the days were

busy, too. His enforced absence of months had not brought improvement to his Oratory. Quickly he took charge again and the old Sunday crowds of boys flocked to listen to him. The Sunday Schools and the night classes were crowded.

Don Bosco was warned to take more heed of his health. But as he explained it afterwards to Father Lemoyne, his biographer: "At first I really meant to obey as far as possible, but when I saw what a great deal there was to do, and that Father Borel and his assistants had as much as they could manage, I could no longer remain idle. I therefore took up all my usual work, and for over twenty-five years I have had no need of doctors or medicines; a circumstance which makes me believe that properly conducted work does not bring anybody harm."

More room was needed, so he rented the rest of the house and now he was able to extend his boy work. The Oratory of St. Francis of Sales was about to receive its first Episcopal Visitation. The Archbishop of Turin, His Grace, Archbishop Fransoni, was to come and great were the preparations of Don Bosco, Mama Margaret, and the boys for that red letter day. It dawned and the Archbishop, mitered and coped and croziered, came into the little chapel that Mama Margaret had beautified to the limit of her slender resources. Everything went perfectly and the Archbishop was seated in the tiny sanctuary. Then came disaster. His Grace rose up to address the round-eyed boys. His miter struck a roof beam and off it came. The Archbishop saved the situation by remarking: "We must be respectful to these boys and address them with uncovered head." So he did. Years later, when the Archbishop was in exile in Lyon, France, he wrote Don Bosco at the time of the building of the new Oratory and Chapel of St. Francis of Sales that he should be sure and make the roof of the chapel high enough. It was this time.

Often Don Bosco had seen the need of giving some waif a night's lodging. Heretofore he had been unable to gratify that need. Now with the whole house his, and Mama Margaret in charge, the opportunity presented itself in this manner. It was the spring of 1847. Don Bosco had been out collecting for his Oratory when at dusk he came up with a gang of boys. He saw at once they were his special kind of boys—ones who called the street their home. As he came closer some of the boys began to cry, "Caw! Caw! Caw!" Around Turin the cry of the crow was an insult sometimes hurled at priests and religious by the liberal-minded and anti-clericals. Don Bosco caught its present significance and smiled. He kept on, decreasing the distance between himself and the crow-imitators. When he was in the midst of the gang, the cawing suddenly ceased and a troubled silence took its place. This priest looked husky—possibly he might not turn the other cheek.

Don Bosco asked pleasantly: "Who are the fellows who were imitating the cry of the crow so excellently?"

None claimed that honor.

"What is the trouble, friends?"

Here one of the older boys said instantly: "If you are a friend, prove it."

"How can I do that, son?"

"Buy all of us a drink."

There was a general laugh.

Don Bosco looked around the street. He saw the sign he wanted.

"Come on, friends," he invited, "there is The Alps Tavern on the corner. I'll treat."

Don Bosco led his suddenly silenced friends into The Alps Tavern. The proprietor knew the priest and his ways and guessed his purpose with this crowd.

Three bottles of wine were ordered and drained.

At the end Don Bosco said: "Now, friends, will you do me a favor?"

"As many as you like, Father," came the shout.

"I only want one. When you cawed at me a little while ago—I let the insult pass. It did not matter. But when some of you use language that blasphemed God, that does matter. It is foolish and ungrateful. You depend on Almighty God for all you have. The favor I ask is that you promise me not to use such language again."

The gang promised. Then when Don Bosco invited them to come to the Oratory, they gladly gave that promise. Already Don Bosco's extraordinary spell was being cast over these boys. As they trooped out of The Alps Tavern, Don Bosco told his friends, "It will be dark soon, you better go home to bed now."

The mention of home brought out the fact that of the twenty boys present a majority had no home to go to. Don Bosco did not need to inquire where these slept. He knew well. In fair weather in the parks; in foul, in stables, with the stable men's permission, or in unfinished houses without anybody's permission.

There and then Don Bosco decided to start his boarding school. "You fellows who have a home, good night. You others, come along with me. I know where I can put you up for the night."

The invitation was gladly heeded. And the twelve walked back to the Valdocco district with the priest. At the Oratory, Mama Margaret helped her son convert the hayloft into a dormitory for the night. Straw sacks made the mattresses and blankets the coverings. Don Bosco had his boy guests kneel down and say an Our Father and a Hail Mary for night prayers. Then he left them to their dreams, and backed down the ladder.

In the morning, when Don Bosco went to the foot of the ladder to call his twelve to breakfast, he discovered they had departed earlier and they had taken the sacks of straw and the blankets as keepsakes of their night's lodging. So the first attempt at putting up his Oratory boys over-night was not a success.

It was in the following May, 1847, that he made his second attempt at giving a stray homeless boy a lodging for the night. Rather, this one sought him out. It had been raining heavily that evening and Don Bosco and Mama Margaret were eating their supper when a knock came at the kitchen door. The priest opened the door and saw a boy, not long past his fourteenth year. He was dripping wet. Could he get something to eat, please?

He could and he did; sharing the simple supper of the mother and son. It came out in the course of the conversation that this boy came from Valsesia, a district some distance from Turin. There had been a little money but it was used all up, looking for work with bricklayers. Then Don Bosco, always thinking of his acquaintances' spiritual progress, questioned: "Have you made your First Communion?"

"Not yet."

"Do you go to Sunday School and Confession?"

"Back in Valsesia, I did, but here in the city, I do not know where to go."

It was the all too common story of the country boy attracted to the city and there neglecting his religion. The rain was still pouring down in torrents and it was out of the question to send this lad out again that night.

Yet Don Bosco remembered his former experience with the twelve.

He said: "If I was sure you were honest I would give you a lodging. I did to some others and they made off with my sacks and blankets."

"Father, I am not a thief," declared the boy.

"I believe you, my child," gently replied Don Bosco and he looked at Mama Margaret.

She nodded, "If you wish, John, we can put this poor child up here in the kitchen."

So with planks placed over some bricks, fresh straw and a blanket, a bed was hastily fashioned. Then Don Bosco questioned the boy about night prayers and discovered that he had forgotten them. Patiently saying phrases of the Hail Mary, he had his little guest repeat them after him. Mama Margaret, with the experience of the thieving dozen still fresh in mind, locked the kitchen door and had her son put the key in his pocket. But the Valsesian boy was grateful and in a few days he had found work and made his home with the Boscos. He was the first Salesian boarder.

The second followed shortly after. One evening Don Bosco found a twelve-year boy, leaning against a tree and crying bitterly. Naturally he stopt and asked the trouble. "Why these tears, sonny?" he inquired.

"Because I do not know what will become of me. My dear Mama was buried this morning."

"But you still have father?"

"He died four years ago. And the landlord turned me out and kept all we had because Mama did not pay the rent."

Something in the boy's manner convinced Don Bosco that this one was telling the truth. "Come with me, my child."

"But I do not know you."

"I am Don Bosco. We shall quickly become friends."

That was a name known to small boys in Turin and the boy came readily. At the home, the priest said to his mother, "Here is another son, Mama Margaret, whom our good God has sent us."

More "sons" were picked up in the streets or came themselves, and by 1848 thirty had been admitted.

These pioneer Salesian boarders put a heavy drain on Don Bosco's thin finances. He walked the streets of Turin begging for his boys. Some of the older boys worked by day. They were apprenticed shoemakers, carpenters, bricklayers. These contributed their mite to the general funds. Always Mama Margaret would say triumphantly when they gave Don Bosco a part of their wages, "Our children earned this money!" Besides the crowds of boys who came each Sunday for Mass and instruction, these boarders went to school and Don Bosco taught them.

When meal times arrived, each one came up to Mama Margaret with his bowl. She filled it, and then the boy found a seat, picnic style—every stone and log and step of the stairs had its particular diner. The well near-by furnished the drink. The meals of necessity were short on food and long on gayety. After the bowl was polished—there were few spoons at first—the boy went to the trough and washed it. Don Bosco would say Grace and end it with his usual jest, "Boys, I wish you all a good appetite." From healthy throats would come bursts of laughter. That was one thing these young charges had in plenty.

Speaking of Don Bosco's own meals, one of these early boarders has written:

> Our soup was his; he had one extra dish, which by his direction his mother made every Sunday, and served daily at dinner and supper, until Thursday evening; on Friday she made another dish, and thus the week was supplied. Generally this famous dish was a pastry, and only required re-heating . . .

In the classroom Don Bosco and his assistants had made a fair beginning of school work for these boys, many of whom needed to start with their ABCs; others, who had picked up some learning, were sorted out into higher classes. A choir thrived. The first Salesian workshops had their beginning. Boys who would have to work by their hands were beginning to be taught various trades. Don Bosco's own boyhood experience of carpentry and iron work stood him in good stead in these classes.

Some of the brighter boys were installed as "Little Masters" and these instructed the younger boys. But the wholesome thing that had entered these Salesian boys' lives for the first time in their neglected years was a Catholic atmosphere. This was most noticeable. Many who visited Don Bosco's converted shed have remarked on this. Here was poverty and at times want, but here also, so visible that it impressed most forcibly those observers, was the joy that goes with innocence and the state of grace.

Regular Confession and frequent Communion was the common practice of Don Bosco's boys. And it was not so common in those days outside the Oratory.

Speaking of Confession there is a charming anecdote that must be inserted here. It was the morning of Confession day and Jemmy, a recent arrival, desired to start all over with a General Confession. With the scrupulousness of a tender conscience, the lad had gone to a corner of the yard and almost filled a copybook with his sins. During the day he lost the sin-laden copybook. That secret writing was only for Don Bosco's eyes in the Confessional and Jemmy after he had searched in vain burst into tears.

With swollen eyes he was led to Don Bosco. A crowd of his school mates clustered around. "Tell me, my little Jemmy, are you ill?" asked the priest solicitously.

"I . . . I've . . . lost . . . my sins!"

A great shout went up from the other lads.

Don Bosco understood Jemmy's statement and he remarked: "Happy boy to have gotten rid of them! For sinless you will surely go to Heaven."

But Jemmy, not understanding, explained:

"Father, they were all written out in a copybook and I've lost that copybook." More abundant tears.

Don Bosco reached into the pocket of his cassock and drew out the missing copybook.

Promptly the tears ceased to flow.

"I found this myself, Jemmy. So take courage, your sins have fallen into safe hands."

Sunshine broke through the clouds and Jemmy with a radiant smile, replied: "O Don Bosco, if I had known you had them I would have laughed and this evening at Confession just said, 'Father, I accuse myself of all the sins you have in your pocket.'"

"Do so, little one, this evening and everything will be all right." Then Don Bosco turned to the listening gang: "Now, you fellows, scatter before I remember something about you."

The boys burst in all directions like bits of an exploding bomb.

Not all the boys at the Oratory were homeless. There was the pathetic case of a youngster, whose father overworked and beat him. This youngster was in the Oratory Sunday School, but at length, the cruelty of his father was too much, and so he fled to Don Bosco's protection. The father chased after him. The boy saw that he could not reach the sanctuary of the Oratory, so he climbed a tree and hid himself there while his angry parent ran on underneath the branches.

Reaching the Oratory, the father demanded of Don Bosco: "Give me back my son."

"But he is not here," truthfully replied the priest.

"He must be. He ran away to you."

"Then very likely you gave him good cause. I tell you again he is not here. And even if he was, what right have you to force yourself into my house and make a disturbance?"

The father threatened to go for the police.

"Go," said Don Bosco, "and when the officer comes I shall lodge a complaint against you, charging mistreatment of your little son."

The father had no desire to have such a charge lodged with the police and he departed grumbling. Some of the Oratory boys had seen the fugitive fleeing and climbing into the tree. Now they told Don Bosco. He, with Mama Margaret and some others, went to the tree and called to the boy. There was no reply. A sharp-eyed Oratory boy discovered the youngster wedged high up in the crotch of two branches. The boy gave no reply to the cries from the ground. Don Bosco, now thoroughly alarmed, sent for a ladder and himself mounted it. He found the boy

unconscious. Cold and fear had done their work. Don
Bosco roused him. At first, he screamed and kicked at his
rescuer. To calm the frightened lad, the priest explained:
"Do not be afraid—look at me. I am Don Bosco, your
friend; if you kick you may hurt me and both of us will
fall." The frightened little fellow finally permitted Don
Bosco to carry him down to the ground where the motherly
arms of Mama Margaret enfolded him. Quickly he was
carried into the house and revived by the fire. He became
a boarder and grew up in the Oratory of St. Francis of
Sales.

During the day the troubles and duties of The Old
Woman Who Lived in a Shoe were trivial compared to
Mama Margaret's. She was everywhere and she was
everything to these boys her son had gathered in from
the highways and the byways of Turin. Some charitable
women had fallen into the habit of coming to the Oratory
to help her. These, all unconsciously, were the pioneer
Salesian Coöperators. At a time when Don Bosco's
resources were at lowest ebb Mama Margaret went to her
few belongings and got out her bridal outfit.

This, after the custom of the peasants of the country,
consisted of dresses of enduring material that mothers
passed down to bridal daughters. There was also some
finer linen and a large gold chain. Mama Margaret looked
her heirloom treasures over. Then she listened to the
shouts that came from the yard below her window. And
the shoutings won. Without telling her priestly son, she
got a woman friend to aid her and soon the dresses were
converted into vestments for the little chapel; the linen
was cut and sewed into surplices and altar cloths; and
then one afternoon Mama Margaret slipt out of the

Oratory and when she returned she had gold coins in place of that cherished gold chain. With this money gold lace and altar ornaments were purchased. It was the widow's mite indeed, but it must have been equally pleasing to Him who saw and understood.

Only once did Mama Margaret refer to this sacrifice and that was in a conversation later with Father Lemoyne. She confided: "I had tears in my eyes when I looked at them for the last time before sending them away or breaking them up; but perceiving my weakness I said: 'Go, dear souvenirs of my husband and parents, you cannot be better applied than for the poor or in God's service.' Having made this sacrifice, I felt peaceful, and would gladly have owned many bridal dresses and much jewelry to devote to the same purpose."

Mama Margaret liked the boisterous youngsters who studied and played around her kitchen. Often she said to her son: "When I had only you and your two brothers, my young family seemed very noisy, a quiet contrast to the uproar of to-day, yet, please God, I shall not mind it more in my old age than when I was young and strong. But, my dear John, always bring as many noisy boys as you like; they will never be too many for me as long as you do them good." No wonder Don Bosco felt able to continue with his arduous boy work, feeling the uplifting influence of such a mother. But sometimes these "noisy boys" lived up to their reputation and then Mama Margaret's patience was stretched to the breaking point.

Years later, in the *Salesian Bulletin* for March, 1881, one of these "noisy boys" retold an incident that brings out Mama Margaret's patience and her son's unique way of dealing with his small charges. We quote:

After the war of 1848 one of our old pupils returned to the Oratory. He had temporarily served in a company of Bersaglieri and naturally we named him "the Sergeant." At our suggestion and with Don Bosco's approval, he formed a little battalion among us to drill. We got two hundred discarded muskets from the Government, and completed our armament with sticks. The Sergeant brought his horn, and, after a short time, our Oratory had at command a brigade whose military instruction would have fitted it for a passage of arms with the National Guard. Our boys were enthusiastically absorbed in these exercises, and would not attend to anything else. Our militia was instrumental in maintaining order in all solemnities, even in the chapel, and attracting many of our former pupils to us again who had been in the war. Mama Margaret, with her usual thrift, reserved a plot of ground at the end of the enclosure as her kitchen garden, where she cultivated parsley, leeks, carrots, sage, and mint. On holidays the Sergeant assembled our little army, divided into two regiments and held a sham battle, gave orders, and decided which was to win and which to lose. In front of the fence we took up our position. He gave the order: "Forward, charge!" Both regiments advanced, shouting, fell back, charged, marched and counter-marched, feigning to use their weapons—guns and sticks. Absence of powder and sound of firing were made up for by the joyous applause of the spectators, which was so noisy that it was a substitute for the cries of the wounded and the roll of artillery.

The battle became so hot that those who were to

surrender, forgetting the watchword, chased those who should have been the victors, and drove them into Mama Margaret's little garden. The fence was broken down and trampled; the leeks and carrots were the dead and wounded. The Sergeant shouted and blew his horn, but the roars of laughter and the clapping of hands from spectators prevented the boys from hearing. When the two banners peacefully joined, hardly any of the little garden remained except its site. Mama Margaret, far from applauding on seeing the devastation, turned to Don Bosco: "Look, look, John, what the Sergeant has done! He has ruined my garden!"

Don Bosco replied smilingly: "Mother, what can you expect from children?"

The Sergeant, mortified at the want of discipline and disregard of authority, was overwhelmed with confusion; however, he ended by drawing from his pocket a bag of burnt sugar, and asking Mama Margaret to distribute it to all the combatants, conquered and conquerors.

As if that was not the last straw to Mama Margaret's patience, it is recorded that she distributed the sugar to the destroyers of her cherished kitchen garden. They were her son's boys and that fact covered a multitude of their sins.

By this time the establishment of Valdocco was on a fairly permanent basis. All Turin knew of its existence and approved of its boy welfare work. Hundreds of boys Don Bosco had taken in, and these hundreds had passed or were passing out of the Oratory ready to take their places as workmen; ready to go into the shops or follow up their various trades, instead of graduating from the street into some Italian prison, where they would take a post graduate course and be released, a greater menace to civil society.

This boy work of Don Bosco had already expanded far beyond the capacity of one man, even a holy genius as Don Bosco was. So, as at the start of all religious congregations, he has been quietly training up others, who shared his enthusiasm for poor boys and looked to this priest as their Guide. These were to be the first members of the future Salesian Society. the first members of the future Salesian Society.

CHAPTER VII

THE GOOD WORK SPREADS

THE Oratory of St. Francis of Sales had become too much of a success. This presented a new problem to Don Bosco. One Sunday he said to Father Borel, "You see the crowds we have at the Oratory! To-day there must have been nearly eight hundred. Why, they hardly had standing room in the chapel! I do not want to send these boys away to the dangers of the street."

Father Borel proposed a migration to larger quarters. To this Don Bosco objected.

"No, not a migration. This site is permanent. But I have been making inquiries among the boys and I find that almost a third of them come from the western section of Turin. Some of them walk two miles or more to attend our classes. So I have been thinking the time has come to open another Oratory in that part of town. In this way we would reduce our numbers here and be able to attract others to the new Oratory."

Far into that Sunday evening the two priests discussed the problem and they went to bed, agreed that another Oratory was imperative. Don Bosco sought Archbishop Fransoni and received permission. Armed with episcopal approbation, he began a search for suitable site. He found the place he wanted on Victor Emmanuel Street, near the River Po. Here was a small house, a miserable shed, with a courtyard between.

A Mrs. Vaglienti owned the property. Don Bosco explained his purpose to this owner, but they could not agree on the annual rental. In the midst of the negotiations a violent thunderstorm arose. A flash of lightning struck near-by. Mrs. Vaglienti jumped in terror. She begged: "Good Don Bosco, if you will pray God to preserve me from this lightning, I will let you have the house for the sum you offer."

"Thank you, madam," Don Bosco replied calmly, "I pray our Lord to protect you now and always."

The lightning ceased and the woman felt reassured. She lived up to her promise and let Don Bosco have the property for the ninety dollars he had offered to pay annually.

Within the week work was begun on transforming this house into an Oratory. Soon a Sunday came when Don Bosco was able to make a welcome announcement to his boys. He couched his news in these words: "My dear boys, when bees become too many for one hive, some of them fly away and form a new family. There are, as you see, so many of us here that we hardly know where to turn. During recreation, every now and then, one of you is knocked down and gets a bloody nose. We are packed together in Chapel like sardines. If we made room by pushing our backs and shoulders against the walls, the place might come down on our heads. What can we do? We must imitate the bees, go somewhere else to open another Oratory, and start another swarm."

There was a beelike buzz of excitement in the hushed audience at this announcement.

Don Bosco continued: "I suppose you boys are all curious to know where the new Oratory is to be, and which of you are going there. Keep quiet and I will tell you in a few words. The Oratory will be planted near the New Gate, a short distance from the iron bridge over the Po. So those who live in that part of the town, will have to go to it, because it will be nearer to their homes, and also because their example will attract other boys in the neighborhood."

"When will it be opened, Father?" an eager boy asked.

"On the eighth of next December. We should like to open our other Oratory on the same feast of Mary Immaculate as we did our first. And it will be called the Oratory of St. Aloysius. There are two reasons for giving it that name. The first is that our boys should have a model of innocence and every other virtue to imitate. The youthful St. Aloysius is exactly the model we want. The second reason is to show our gratitude to our good Archbishop, Monsignor Aloysius Fransoni, who loves us so much, and who is so kind in putting us under his special protection. I hope, boys, that you are pleased with the news that I have just told you."

There was no doubt about the reception that this announcement received. And so on the Feast of the Immaculate Conception, 1847, the Oratory of St. Aloysius commenced its career of usefulness. Snow was falling as the boys gathered. They looked on this as a happy omen, as snow had fallen three years ago when the Oratory of St. Francis of Sales opened. Father Hyacinth Carpano, a new helper of Don Bosco in his boy work, was made first Director of this second Salesian Oratory. Don Bosco multiplied his activities and often visited his other "hive of bees."

Eighteen months later the numbers forced another swarming and the third Oratory—that of the Guardian Angels—was opened in the Vanchiglia quarter of Turin

The year 1849 was one of political trouble for the Holy Father and he had to flee to Gaeta. While His Holiness was there Don Bosco's boys donated what they could to Peter's Pence. Trifling was the sum, but Pius IX was so touched by the boys' charity that he sent, through Cardinal Antonelli, his Secretary of State, a pair of Rosary beads, blessed by himself, for the boys of each Oratory. When Don Bosco distributed these beads there was great rejoicing.

It was at this period, when anticlericalism was raging, that attempts were made on the life of Don Bosco. One Sunday afternoon, when he was preaching to his boys in the Valdocco Chapel, a man suddenly appeared at the open window and raising a pistol, fired at the priest. The bullet passed under Don Bosco's arm and buried itself in the wall beyond. Instant panic reigned. Don Bosco quieted the boys and then told them:

"See, Our Lady, Help of Christians, has protected me." He looked ruefully at the tear in his cassock and added with a smile: "But it is too bad that she did not protect you, my poor cassock. For you are the only one that I have!"

Other opposition arose from some undesirable neighbors in the Valdocco section. These found that the good Don Bosco was doing with the boys and young men was seriously interfering with their designs. This opposition became dangerous. One day a man, seemingly mad, flourishing a grim-looking butcher's knife, came running at Don Bosco. Taken by surprise, he had only time to run into his room and lock the door. The madman took up his watch in the corridor. Some of the older Oratory boys threw stones and sticks at him from a safe distance, while Mama Margaret, when the excitement was at its height, rushed out and found a policeman. He came and, disarming the madman, took him away to prison. The next day, an anticlerical magistrate released the would-be assassin on the grounds that Don Bosco had said he pardoned him. What Don Bosco had actually said was, "I pardon him as a Christian, but as a citizen and the head of an institution I claim the protection of the laws of my country."

A gentleman, friendly to Don Bosco, went to the released madman and asked: "Why did you try to kill Don Bosco?"

He was told very frankly, "Because sixteen dollars were paid me to feign madness and stab him."

The friend had an idea. "Sixteen dollars to kill Don Bosco! Well, what would you do if I gave you thirty-two dollars not to injure him?"

The "gunman" thought for a moment and replied: "Just double! Then I shall guard him when necessary." He was paid the money and for a time became Don Bosco's bodyguard.

But there were still evil-minded men and women in the Valdocco neighborhood who disapproved of Don Bosco's good influence over the young. They attempted effective means to remove the troublesome priest. On a moonless night a rough-looking man appeared at the Festive Oratory gate. He seemed to be in great distress and begged Don Bosco to come and hear the confession of a dying man. Prudent Mama Margaret did not like the looks of the messenger and she said so. But her son was a priest and he went with the man. As soon as he was out of sight Mama Margaret called four of the larger boys and told them to arm themselves with sticks and to follow. Willingly they did. Running along they came up to Don

Bosco and the messenger. When all came to the house of the dying man, two of the boys remained before the house and the more venturesome two went up the stairs after the priest and stationed themselves outside the door of the sick room.

Don Bosco walked calmly across the room and his experienced eyes told him at once that this dying man appeared healthy looking. Next second the candle was blown out. Don Bosco turned in the dark to help the man relight the candle and that movement fortunately saved his life. For the man's club, aimed at the priest's head, missed and Don Bosco received the blow on his shoulder. He remembered where the chair was and quickly seizing it, covered his head and groped for the door.

Outside the two young guards heard the noise. They promptly burst open the door. There was Don Bosco with the chair caged over his head, and the two men trying to club him down. With the arrival of timely assistance, the attempt on the priest's life ceased. The boys helped their beloved Director downstairs. Back once more in the shelter of the Oratory it was discovered that Don Bosco's left thumb had been badly mashed by a blow from a club. Mama Margaret dressed it and told her son meanwhile what she thought of priests who went out with strange men after dark to strange houses.

It was after this that Grigio (The Gray One) came on the scene. This was a huge gray dog. His breed was unknown, but those who were privileged to see him thought he might be a Great Dane. What is quite clear is that Grigio was a one-man dog and his "one man" was Don Bosco.

One of the Oratory boys of those days has left us an interesting account of this mysterious dog. He says:

Sometimes Don Bosco returned from Turin at a late hour, due to sick calls or other duties, and pursued his way to Valdocco without a thought as to personal danger. The ground which he had to traverse, now occupied with buildings and lighted with gas, was then broken, intersected by quagmires, and bordered here and there by thick hedges, effectual hiding places for malefactors. One night, returning home later than usual, he saw a huge dog approach, and felt alarmed. But the animal seemed so gentle, wagged his tail, and turned to walk beside Don Bosco. The priest caressed him and all fear vanished. The dog escorted Don Bosco to the Oratory, but refused to enter; afterwards, whenever late in coming home, on one side or the other of the lonely way, the Gray One appeared.

Frequently Mama Margaret, when her son was late, sent some of us grown pupils to meet him. I have gone and have seen him and his dog walking along side by side on several occasions. Three times to my certain knowledge Grigio saved his life. One foggy, dark winter's night, Don Bosco took a short cut from the Consolata to Cottolengo Institute. At a corner of the road he perceived two men, regulating their pace with his, evidently with evil intentions, so he hastened toward an inhabited house for refuge. But he was overtaken; one of the men threw a cloak over his head. He tried to cry for help, but could not, as he was immediately gagged with a handkerchief. He felt hopeless of escape, when a sudden terrible howl was heard, less like the growl of a dog than the grumbling of an infuriated bear. This was Grigio, who sprang first on one of the wretches, then on the other, biting, growling, howling, snarling, jumping, and ended by throwing one down. Both miscreants, terrified, asked pardon and exclaimed: "Call off your dog, call him quickly, or we shall be torn to pieces."

"Yes, my friends," said Don Bosco, who had extricated himself from the gag, "on condition you go your way, and let me go mine."

"Yes, yes, we are off, but hold your dog." Don Bosco called Grigio and the men ran away.

The former pupil of Don Bosco related another exploit of this large dog, who resembled Rin-tin-tin of movie fame.

On another occasion Grigio defended Don Bosco from a formidable band of paid assassins. When at midnight, passing through Milan Place—now Emmanuel Philibert Place—he observed a man following him, armed with a large cudgel, and hastened with the hope of reaching the Oratory safely. He was already at the top of the declivity when lower down he saw a group of men; then he waited for the one behind, whom he threw down. The man's comrades surrounded Don Bosco with raised sticks; the faithful Grigio appeared beside his protégé, snarling and springing about in such fury that the wretches, terrified, besought Don Bosco to quiet the dog, and vanished into the darkness. Don Bosco's faithful four-footed guardian escorted him to the door of the Oratory.

But the following incident, of quite a different nature, seems to reveal that this singular dog was inspired with marvelous intuition. Contrary to custom, Don Bosco forgot an important commission in Turin. He was preparing to start in the evening to repair his forgetfulness when Mama Margaret tried to dissuade him; he endeavored to reassure her, and opened the door to go out, when he found Grigio stretched full length on the threshold. "Oh! so much the better; we shall be two instead of one, and able to defend ourselves." He called and called, but the dog would not stir; and when Don Bosco tried to pass, growled. Twice Don Bosco tried to go out, but in vain; Grigio prevented him. Mama Margaret then said, "You see, my son, the dog has more sense than you; do mind him!" On the repeated refusal of Grigio to make way Don Bosco had to return to his room. A few minutes later a neighbor came warning him to be on his guard, as some ill-looking men were lurking about."

This Grigio was the cause of considerable conversation among the Oratory boys. Many had seen him, escorting their Director when he needed police protection, but when they went searching for the huge dog's home they were disappointed. He did not live in the Valdocco section and he was never seen, except as armed guardian of Don Bosco.

The one time the boys did see him "close up" was when the attacks on Don Bosco's life fell off. Here we quote from Father Bonetti:

After the times had grown calmer, Grigio made Don Bosco a sort of congratulatory visit. As the large gray dog made his way through the front yard some of the boys playing there undertook to keep him out—these had never seen him before. But Grigio dodged them, and got into the house. Don Bosco was at supper with some friends. The dog walked solemnly around the room eyeing each one, and then went straight up to Don Bosco, who patted him and offered him food—bread, meat, soup and water by turns. But Grigio would touch nothing, not even sniff at anything. Don Bosco said: "Well then, Grigio, what do you want?" The dog pushed his head under Don Bosco's hands and received his caresses, gazing fondly into his face, wagging his tail, and then he turned and went out the door with his grateful friend's blessing.

That was the last but one of Grigio's mysterious appearances. Years passed and he had become a memory to the Oratory boys—a green memory, because Don Bosco often spoke of him and used him in illustration in his sermons, so that even the newcomers to the Oratories felt that they knew Grigio.

The last appearance of "The Gray One" was as sudden and mysterious as the first. It was years later, on the evening of February 12, 1883. Don Bosco was on a visit to his old home at Becchi and in company with some friends he went from Murialdo to Moncucco to visit an old acquaintance, Luigi Moglia. It got dark before they reached their destination and they had yet to pass by some farms and vineyards that were guarded by savage dogs. To add to their dangers it began to rain heavily and the unknown road turned to a muddy river bottom. Several times the party wandered off the road and at length, Don Bosco exclaimed: "If only I had my faithful Grigio along, we would—"

No sooner had the priest uttered this heartfelt wish than a huge gray shadow came out of the surrounding black wall. One of the party cried out in alarm: "Look out for that beast!"

A smile spread over Don Bosco's features. He recognized the "beast" instantly. "That's my Grigio. Come here, boy. Where have you been all these years?"

The Gray One came up to Don Bosco, wagging his tail affectionately. He licked the priest's hand. The others had halted at a prudent distance and Father Durando asked if it was really Grigio.

"Yes," said Don Bosco, "The same size, color, and he certainly recognizes me. But I know a better proof." He addressed the gray dog. "If you really are my faithful old Grigio, you will lead us out of this quagmire."

The huge dog at once started off, stopt after a few steps and looked back, as if to say, "My dear Master, you and your party follow me and there will be no cause for worry."

Follow him all gladly did and they experienced his protection, for along the way when they came to a farm, two fierce dogs leapt out. But Grigio was on them in an instant. There were twin howls in the darkness and Grigio returned to his party, again waving a victorious tail. So all came to the home of Luigi Moglia, where Don Bosco and his friends were warmly welcomed. All through supper the family plied Don Bosco with questions about the gray dog that lay at rest outside the door. Don Bosco could only reply that he had uttered a wish for the presence of Grigio and Grigio had materialized.

At the end of the meal, Signor Moglia said, "That faithful gray dog must also have his supper." And he himself gathered up a plate of bones. But when he went to the door, there was no trace of the Gray One. He had never been seen in that neighborhood before and never was he seen there again. Nor at any future time did anyone ever see that large dog, whose presence was enough to excite comment. This Grigio of Don Bosco is a huge gray mystery. Was he a real dog or was he Don Bosco's Guardian Angel in canine form? Some day in the other world we shall know.

To this period belongs another remarkable—shall we call it?—experience. Not dogs this time but boys.

It happened in May, 1855 that Don Bosco, besides his many other duties, undertook to preach an eight-day Retreat to the juvenile prisoners at the Turin jail called the "Generala." Over three hundred boys and youths made this Retreat. All of them had been committed by the Court for offenses, minor and more serious. It was a Reformatory and the type of boy who attended the Spiritual Exercises were not the white-collared Sunday School type.

However, they were boys and they fell under the kindly influence of Don Bosco. They listened at first with enforced attention, but soon this master of the boy heart had won their attention and their love. The effects of the Retreat were visible to the keepers long before the last day. On that morning the hundreds of youthful prisoners, having made their peace with Jesus in the Confessional, came up to the prison chapel and received the One Who knew and pardoned and loved them. Don Bosco searched his mind to find some way to reward these zealous Retreatants and he hit on a novel plan. He went to the Warden and made this proposal. "Mr. Warden, will you permit me to take these boys for a day's outing into the country?"

The Warden was what some might call "hard-boiled" and he looked pityingly at the priest who sat by his desk. "Don Bosco, if I listened to your astonishing proposal, I might as well close down this Reformatory. By nightfall, none of these young criminals would be in sight and it would take most of the policemen and soldiers in Turin weeks to round them all up. I might as well go down to the Zoo and let out all the wild birds, bidding them to be sure and return by five P.M. No, of course, I couldn't consider such a ridiculous proposition."

Don Bosco replied: "Mr. Warden, you are mistaken in your estimate of these boys. They have just made a good Retreat and I believe they are in the state where they belong—in the state of grace. I know how to treat them. Before we start I shall put each of them on his honor to return at the end of the day. There will be no need of sending a single policeman along. They will all be back. This I promise you."

"The honor of thieves and of future cutthroats!" stormed the Warden. Don Bosco listened and then he repeated his request. Finally, the Warden, more to rid himself of this mad cleric, promised to forward the remarkable request to Signor Rattazzi, the Minister of State, under whose Department the "Generala" was.

The Warden received the shock of his life when the request came back with "Granted" written at the bottom of the page by Minister Rattazzi. Still doubting what his eyes told him, the Warden went personally to the Minister and learned, "I wish the experiment to be tried."

The juvenile prisoners were wild with joy when, the evening before the outing, Don Bosco assembled them and said: "To-morrow we have permission to have a picnic at Stupinigi." This was a village about four miles south-west of Turin. "I needn't tell you boys," continued the priest, when silence had been restored, "that I have given my word of honor that all who go on this picnic will return to this Reformatory to-morrow evening."

Here Don Bosco was interrupted by one of the older boys threatening: "If any of these fellows tries to run away I'll run after him and tear him to pieces." Similar prophecies of dire swift punishment were uttered by other older boys. Don Bosco said that he did not believe there would be any need of maiming any members of the picnic party. He knew the hearts of these boys and he left them, confident that those he conducted to Stupinigi would keep faith with him.

Such an unique outing could not be kept secret. Many watched with dubious eyes. We can almost see the Warden, gazing on the backs of his three hundred next morning, and shaking his head sadly. So they sallied forth like any troop of boys, intent on the joys of the country-side. A pack horse, loaded down with picnic food, led the procession through the streets of Turin. Don Bosco joined different groups en route. The Reformatory was as a thing forgotten.

At Stupinigi were the Royal Gardens of King Charles Albert. Here the parish priest, Father E. Amaretti, who believed in Don Bosco and his boy work, joined the picnic party. It is unnecessary to say that a good time was had by all. And all too swiftly the sun began to sink in the west and it was time to hike back to Turin and gray walls. It was unnecessary to "tear anybody to pieces" for every last "juvenile delinquent" walked back to the Reformatory.

Don Bosco's prison picnic was talked of next day all over the city. It brought to public attention more forcibly than eloquent words the hold he had over boys. What was more remarkable, these boys were not his Oratory boys, who knew him intimately and lived with him, but boys and young men under twenty-one, who only met him occasionally and at that under unfavorable conditions.

CHAPTER VIII

MAMA MARGARET GOES HOME

THE Fall of 1856 had in store for the Oratory of St. Francis of Sales a heavy sorrow. Mama Margaret, busy attending to the boys' needs, fell ill. There was no need to warn the boys to walk softly in the neighborhood of that sick room. It became a "Hospital Zone—All Unnecessary Noises Prohibited."

Then the news spread that Mama Margaret had pneumonia, and her boys thronged the chapel and knelt especially before the Lady Altar. Don Bosco's brother Joseph came from his farm at Castelnuovo. Father Borel heard her Confession and brought her Holy Viaticum. Before receiving Extreme Unction Mama Margaret said to her priestly son: "John, once I helped you to receive the Last Sacraments of our Holy Religion, and now you must help your mother."

Sorrowfully, Don Bosco nodded assent. And he assisted at the bedside while his mother was anointed. She received the Last Sacraments calmly. For she fully realized the seriousness of her condition. To each of her sons she gave suitable farewell advice. She told Joseph to raise his sons farmers, unless they showed a vocation for the priesthood. And she begged him "to do for the Oratory all that you are able. The Blessed Virgin then will bless you and your family and make you and them happy all the days of your life."

Then turning to Don Bosco, Mama Margaret showed that the boys were uppermost in her mind. "What I am about to tell you, John, I say with that same sincerity that I would in Confession, in order that you may know the state of the Oratory. Have great confidence in those who will work with you in the vineyard of the Lord, but only in those things that you are sure are for the glory of God. Be careful, for many will seek their own interests rather than the glory of God. I must depart and leave the things of the Oratory in the hands of others. It will be a change that will have displeasing consequences, but Our Lady will not fail to guide your affairs. Do not seek either elegance or splendor in your works. Seek the glory of God, but have poverty as your basis. You have many that love poverty in others, but not in themselves. The more efficacious teaching is to do that which is commanded to others. Preserve your family in the proper state—poverty. That will do it a great good."

Then she spoke to Don Bosco of many intimate things of the Oratory and showed such a shrewd insight into human nature that her son was amazed. She promised if, by the mercy of God, she should go to Heaven, she would pray unceasingly for the Oratory. In her delirium her thoughts were on those poor boys whom she had made her own children. And the boys were crowding the chapel, as they had done some years before when their beloved Don Bosco lay at the point of death. But this time their prayers were to be heard differently.

Mama Margaret's work was over. That last earthly night, John Bosco and his brother watched at the bedside. Joseph was the calmer. When Mama Margaret noticed her John's unconcealed grief, she motioned for him to stoop low over the pillow and she whispered: "Johnnie dear, God knows how much I have loved you in the course of my life. I hope to be able to love you more in Heaven. I have a peaceful conscience. I have done my duty in all that I have been able. Perhaps, it seemed that I have been too harsh in some things, but it is not so. It was the voice of duty commanding and imposing. Tell our dear boys that I have worked for them and have a motherly love for all of them. I recommend myself to their prayers and ask them to offer up at least one Communion for my soul."

Here the good Mama Margaret's tears overcame her and Don Bosco broke down, too.

"Go, my dearest John," she ordered, "go away, because you make me sorrowful to see you so afflicted. Besides, you suffer more seeing me in these last moments. Good-by, John. Remember that this life consists in suffering. True pleasures will be found in Heaven. Go into your room and pray for me."

Don Bosco hesitated, but as there did not appear to be any immediate danger of his mother dying, he finally left the room, leaving Father Alasonatti on watch.

Then occurred several strange things. When Don Bosco reached his room, he attempted to light his lamp. Three times he tried and each time it went out. His thoughts immediately turned to his Mother's numbered minutes. At length the lamp stayed lit and by its light he gazed affectionately at the picture of Mama Margaret that hung near his bed. It blurred as he prayed. Finally, as he had promised her, he undressed to retire. Then he noticed his mother's picture again. It had turned its face toward the wall!

Don Bosco got up, saying to himself, "I fear that is the sign that Heaven sends me of the immediate departure of poor Mother for eternity!" He returned to Mama Margaret's bedroom. She noticed him at once, and motioned him to depart and not witness her agony. When he did not leave, she said: "John, you are not able to endure this sight."

Don Bosco was weeping heavily and in a broken voice he protested: "Mother, it is not the part of an affectionate son to abandon you at this time."

Mama Margaret was silent for a short while. Then with difficulty she spoke: "Johnnie, Johnnie, I ask you for a favor and it is the last that I ask of you. My suffering is doubled seeing you suffer. I have enough help here." She indicated the other priests and her sister, who were in the room. "You go away and pray for me. I ask nothing else. Good-by, Johnnie."

So the good son of a saintly mother obediently left the chamber.

About three o'clock—it was the morning of November 25, 1856—Don Bosco rose from his knees. He had recognized the step of his brother, coming to his door. One look at Joseph's face and John knew his beloved Mama Margaret had become more powerful than ever to help his boy work. Later in the morning, when the weeping boys gathered around him he said: "We have lost our mother, but I am sure that she will help us from her place in Paradise. She was a saint."

We who know anything of this illiterate peasant woman, who was mother to countless motherless little ones, echo the eulogy of her holy son—"She was a saint!"

CHAPTER IX

SALESIAN STARTS

ONE of the principles of Don Bosco was to leave most of his worries to Mary, Help of Christians. That Our Lady did this favorite son's worrying is notably illustrated in the beginnings of the Congregation that Don Bosco was to found. We have seen the one-room Oratory develop into three Oratories. Rather, four, for another Oratory had been opened at Mirabello in 1863. Many people interested in the remarkably successful boy work of this holy Turin priest, suggested that he take steps to put his works on a solid and lasting basis.

But it was a conversation with the anti-clerical Minister of the King, Urban Rattazzi, that started Don Bosco on the direct path to be the Founder of the Salesian Congregation that we know to-day. It came about in this way. One day in 1857 Minister Rattazzi, who from time to time had shown himself friendly to Don Bosco's boy works, sent for the priest and said to him bluntly: "I hope, Don Bosco, that you will live for many years to educate the hundreds of boys you have with you, but you are mortal, like all of us, and if you were suddenly called away, what would become of your work? Have you adopted any means to secure the permanency of your Institution?"

To these questions coming from the Minister of State, who had been instrumental in suppressing Religious Orders in the Kingdom of Piedmont and even in driving the religious beyond the country's borders, Don Bosco was somewhat taken aback. "To tell you the truth, Your Excellency, I have not thought of dying so soon. I have thought of getting present help, but not of securing the carrying on the work of the Oratories after my death. Now that you have mentioned the matter, how would you advise me to go about putting my Oratories on a safe footing?"

Promptly this anti-clerical Minister outlined his plan. "You should select a certain number of ecclesiastics and laymen, form a society under certain rules, and instill in them your spirit and methods."

Don Bosco's famous smile came into action. "Does Your Excellency believe it is possible to found such a religious society in these days?"

The Minister brushed this objection aside. "I am fully acquainted with the Law of Suppression and also with its scope. Your society before the government would be nothing more than an association of free citizens, united and living together, and having the same benevolent scope in view. The government will not oppose such a society."

"You have given me an idea," said Don Bosco, and he went back to the Valdocco Oratory.

The suggestion of forming a religious congregation, coming from such an irreligious source, spurred on Don Bosco. He consulted ecclesiastical friends and he interviewed laymen who had shown an interest in his boys. Then he set definitely about forming a distinct society, whose principal object should be the care of neglected boys. Rules were drafted.

When the news that Don Bosco was thinking of forming a society of helpers, some of his coadjutors, priests, seminarians, and older Oratory boys, asked to join. Soon an infant congregation of about twelve took shape. Of these, some lived at home and came to the Oratories on Sundays and feast days to help in the boy work. Others moved to the Oratory of St. Francis of Sales and began living in common with Don Bosco as their Superior. As yet this was a civil society. Don Bosco discussed the plans with Father Cafasso, his Confessor, and that holy man approved and advised laying the whole matter before His Grace. But at this time Archbishop Fransoni was living in exile at Lyon, France. Accordingly, Don Bosco wrote his Archbishop at length. Back came the full episcopal approval. But the Bishop suggested that Don Bosco take his plans to Rome and lay them at the feet of the Sovereign Pontiff.

So on February 21, 1858, Don Bosco, accompanied by his secretary, Michael Rua, a former Oratory boy now in his theological studies, who was to be his successor as General of the Salesians, paid his first visit to the Eternal City. One cannot walk in on the Pope, so Don Bosco spent the time waiting for his audience in visiting the various places where boy work was being carried on in Rome. Then on the evening of March 8 he received the following most welcome notice:

> The Reverend John Bosco is hereby informed that His Holiness has been pleased to arrange for an audience to-morrow, the 9th of March, between twelve and one o'clock.

When Don Bosco was ushered into the presence of Pius IX, His Holiness recalled the Peter's Pence that the Oratory boys had sent him, saying: "When I think of those boys I still feel touched by the remembrance of those six dollars they sent me at Gaeta. Poor boys, they deprived themselves of their scant allowances; it was a great sacrifice for them!"

Then Don Bosco described his boy work in Turin. His Holiness listened attentively and asked: "If you were to die, what would become of your work?"

At this favorable opening Don Bosco, presented his Archbishop's approval and explained his own plans for fellow workers. Pius IX exhorted Don Bosco to draw up his Rules according to his plan and made some important suggestions. That first audience ended by the Pope giving Don Bosco and his boys the Papal blessing. With the Pope's approval of his little congregation, Don Bosco was of a mind to return to Turin at once. But Pius IX sent him an invitation to give one of his wholesome Retreats to the youths held in the State prisons. Naturally Don Bosco accepted this invitation as a Papal command.

Don Bosco had two more private audiences with the Pope and in the last one, Pius IX said to Don Bosco: "Now isn't there something more you wish?"

"Your Holiness has granted all I wish and it only remains for me to thank you again."

"Come, come, Don Bosco, there is something else you want?"

Don Bosco shook his head.

"What? Don't you wish to make your boys merry when you return to them?"

"Why, certainly, Your Holiness," was the only answer Don Bosco could give.

"Wait a minute then." Pius IX went to a small safe and opening it took out twenty-five gold coins, equivalent to one hundred and twenty-five dollars, explaining, "Take these with you and give your boys a treat in my name."

So Don Bosco came back to Turin and Valdocco,

delighted with his first Roman visit and its successful preliminary approval of his rules. The boys of the Oratories shouted and gave the local equivalent for the locomotive yell for His Holiness, when they learned of his treat. They had cast the bread of their Peter's Pence on the waters and it had literally come back a hundredfold.

Speaking of treats for the Oratory boys, there was another extraordinary treat. This really occurred previous to the Papal one.

There was a pious custom at the Oratories, introduced by Don Bosco from the earliest days, and this custom was to have the boys make a Monthly Preparation for the grace of a happy death. After the exercises were over in the chapel, Don Bosco declared a walk to a neighboring cemetery to pray for the dead. This was shortly after All Souls' Day. On the boys' return Don Bosco promised them a feast of roast chestnuts. There were three sacks of chestnuts in the kitchen, but the cook roasted only a small quantity of these chestnuts. The first of the Oratory boys to return from the cemetery was Joseph Buzzetti. With his mind on the promised chestnut feed, he rushed to the kitchen and seeing only a small kettle full of the nuts over the fire, promptly told the cook that there were not enough for twenty boys there and chestnuts had been promised to all the six hundred and fifty boys. His remonstrances were cut short by the arrival of the vanguard of the hungry chestnut seekers. With visions of the coming disappointment of his chums written large on his face, Joseph emptied all the roast chestnuts into a basket and brought them to Don Bosco, who had taken up his place outside the chapel to make the promised distribution.

At once Don Bosco started to fill the cap of each boy. Finally Joseph Buzzetti intervened: "What are you doing,

Father! We have not enough for all at the rate you are giving them out."

"Indeed we have. I sent three sacks to the kitchen."

"That's all right, but the cook only roasted these we have in this basket," and Joseph ruefully looked at the diminished supply. He evidently had not received his share yet.

When Don Bosco understood the situation, he calmly said: "Well, Joe, let us keep on giving the same amount to each hungry lad as long as we have some."

Joseph shook his head and whispered the sad news to some particular friends of his down the line. There were, at least, over four hundred boys awaiting their share of roast chestnuts. Bad news, especially in regard to eatables, is easily broadcast and the shouts gave place to uneasy silence. Don Bosco sent for the rest of the chestnuts. He saw that Joseph had told him aright. He looked at the disappointed countenances of the boys crowding around him and then he bowed his head in silent prayer.

Joseph heard him say, "I have promised this treat to my boys and I shall not disappoint them." Picking up the large perforated ladle, he recommenced to fill the outstretched caps.

Joseph Buzzetti, standing beside the priest, looked and his eyes began to blaze with excitement. For Don Bosco continued to pass out chestnuts and the amount in the basket remained the same! Joseph was not the only one who noticed that something out of the ordinary was happening. The rumor spread that a modern version of the multiplication of the loaves and the fishes was taking place in the yard. The boys forgot to eat their chestnuts, while they watched Don Bosco calmly portioning out of that basket a capful of roast chestnuts to each of the remaining four hundred boys.

When the last Oratory boy had had his share, a great shout went up from the hundreds of boys, "Don Bosco is a saint!" "Don Bosco is a saint!"

In vain the Director of the Oratory tried to still that vociferous truth. Don Bosco handed the basket to Joseph Buzzetti and motioned him to carry it back to the kitchen. Joseph saw that just one portion of chestnuts was in the bottom of the basket. Evidently Our Lady, Help of Christians, had thoughtfully decided that her priestly favorite was entitled to his capful.

In memory of this miracle of the chestnuts, the custom came in to give the boys at the Salesian Oratories throughout the world roasted chestnuts on All Souls' Day.

On another occasion—this was a Feast Day—all the boys were to receive. Don Bosco was saying the Mass. When it came to Communion time, he opened the tabernacle. The sacristan almost had an attack of heart failure as he suddenly remembered he had forgotten to put out another ciborium to be consecrated, and there were only a few hosts in the ciborium. The first of the boys were kneeling at the rails. The sacristan saw Don Bosco take the cover off the ciborium and notice its contents. He seemed confused for a moment. Then he raised his eyes to Heaven and prayed. At the conclusion of his prayer he calmly turned around and began to give Holy Communion. Each of the six hundred and fifty boys received Communion from that partially filled ciborium. When Don Bosco was questioned about this remarkable multiplication, he admitted it and replied that Divine Goodness looked after the boys.

Among the characteristics that drew boys to Don Bosco

was his knack of preaching to them.   Many stories are told
of his oratory, suitable for the teen age.   Once when he
had preached on Scandal, as his custom was, he recreated
with the boys who came Sundays to the Oratories.   Wishing to drive in the lesson on these less frequent attendants
at the Oratory he questioned a group on the subject of the
morning's sermon.   Silence greeted his question.   He
asked one, another—the fifth.   All had forgotten the topic.

"Poor me!" exclaimed Don Bosco, "I must have been
preaching in Greek this morning, or, possibly, you were
dreaming."

More silence from the group.   Finally a small voice
piped up: "Don Bosco, I remember something."

"Well, that is an encouraging sign.   What do you
remember, buddy?"

"I remember the story of the monkeys."

And the little fellow, at the priest's urging, began to
repeat the anecdote.   As it is a good example of Don
Bosco's methods of illustrating his talks, it is inserted.

Once upon a time, a pedlar was overtaken by night
in a woods far from any town or village.   It was an
evening in summer.   The moon shone in the heavens
and the stars twinkled, and the poor pedlar, weary
and worn out after a hard day's tramping from one
place to another, chose a sheltered spot near a giant
tree, where he decided to pass the night.   In order to
shield his head from the falling dew, he opened his
pack of wares and extracted one of the nightcaps, and
putting it on his head, he lay down and was soon fast
asleep.   Now the branches of the tree under which
the pedlar was taking his rest, were alive with
monkeys—in fact, it was in monkey land.   The little

creatures had watched the man below in attentive silence, and no sooner had he dropped off to sleep than one of their number quietly descended from his perch to the pack. Thrusting his paw inside, he drew out a nightcap, and without more ado, gravely donned his trophy and then returned to take up his position as formerly. One after another his brethren proceeded to do likewise, until there was not a nightcap left. The pedlar slept soundly, and, for the first time in their lives, the inhabitants of monkey land slept with nightcaps on. Meantime dawn came, and the sun had hardly risen above the horizon, when our friend, the pedlar, roused himself. Great, indeed, was his surprise and his annoyance on finding that all his stock of nightcaps had disappeared from his pack. "Thieves have been here!" he cried, "and ruined me!"

On a closer examination, however, he became doubtful as to his first conclusion, reflecting that had thieves been there they would have carried off everything. The poor man was sorely perplexed. At this point he heard a slight noise above, and on looking up he was dumbfounded to see all the monkeys in nightcaps.

"Ah, there are the robbers!" he cried; and he at once began to try to frighten them by shouting at them and pelting them with stones, in order to make them give up the stolen goods; but the monkeys ran from branch to branch, and seemed disinclined to gratify him. Several hours thus passed; the poor pedlar had shouted himself hoarse, and tired himself with his unusual exertions, yet all to no purpose.

Mad with rage, and hardly knowing what he was doing, he seized the nightcap, which he had worn until then, and flung it on the ground in despair. At this sight, the monkeys felt themselves irresistibly impelled to do likewise, and a shower of nightcaps descended to cheer the heart of the distracted pedlar.

And Don Bosco concluded his anecdote by observing, "My sons, boys act more or less in the same fashion as these monkeys. When they see others doing what is right, they feel drawn to imitate them; when what is evil, the attraction to do likewise is still greater."

It is a natural step from monkeys to elephants and that brings to mind the sermon of Don Bosco that has become known as "The Elephant Dream." It was in 1862 that he preached it to the boys. As it is an excellent illustration of his boy sermons it is given in practically Don Bosco's own words.

I dreamt, my dear boys, that it was a Sunday afternoon during recreation and you were all enjoying yourselves in many different ways. It seemed to me that I was in my room with Professor Vallauri. We had been discussing for a good while religion and other topics, when I suddenly heard somebody knocking at the door. I ran to see who it was. It was my mother, dead already six years, who almost out of breath was saying to me: "Come and see. Come and see." "What is the matter?" I asked. "Come. Come," Mama Margaret replied. At her insistence, I stepped out on the balcony and what did I see! In the playground with the boys there was an elephant of enormous size. "How did he get here!" I exclaimed. "Let us hurry downstairs." I looked at the Professor in amazement. He was also looking at me, so that we both looked at each other as if to ask how that enormous wild beast could have entered the yard. We ran downstairs. Many boys gathered around us. It seemed that the elephant was tame and mild. He was amusing himself walking around among the boys and caressing them with his huge trunk. He was so intelligent that he obeyed all orders as if he had been trained and brought up at the Oratory since he was born. He was always followed and petted by a great crowd. Not everybody was around him, though. I saw that the greater part of you were frightened and were running here and there in search of a place where you could remain away from the elephant. Finally you ran into the church. I also was going to enter through the back door, but passing by the statue of the Blessed Virgin, I touched the hem of her mantle and she raised her right arm. The Professor did the same thing on the other side and she moved her left. I was amazed and did not know how to explain the wonder.

Now it was time for services in church, and you, my dear boys, went in. I also entered and saw the elephant standing in back of the church by the door. Vespers were sung and after the sermon I went to the altar in order to give Benediction of the Blessed Sacrament. But at the most solemn moment, when everybody was bowing in adoration to the Holy of Holies, I saw the elephant in the middle of the aisle in the back of the church, kneeling and bowing too, but in a different manner from you boys. His head faced the door. At the end of the service I was going to go right out in the yard in order to observe what would happen, but somebody who wanted to talk to me delayed me for a while.

When I came out, the boys were in the yard. The elephant having come out of the church went into the yard also. At the same time the boys in the yard were in a procession. They had at their head a banner with the inscription, "Holy Mary, Comforter of the Afflicted."

Then suddenly I saw the elephant, which before had looked so calm and gentle, become wild and rush in the midst of the boys. Trumpeting, and grasping the boys nearest to him with his trunk, he threw them up high in the air and dashed them to the ground. Then he would trample on them, making a horrible slaughter. Nevertheless, those who were thus treated were not killed, although they were wounded severely. Everybody tried to save himself; some were screaming, others crying, more were calling for help. On the other hand, horrible to say, some of the boys, spared by the elephant, instead of helping their companions, had even made alliance with the monster in order to get him some more victims.

While this was going on and while I was still standing near the statue, it took life, enlarged itself and became a living person. Our Lady spread out her mantle on which were embroidered many magnificent inscriptions. And this mantle enlarged itself too, so that it became big enough to cover all those who sought to take refuge under it.

At first, a large number of the best boys ran to that refuge. But the Blessed Virgin, seeing that many did not hasten to her, cried out in a loud voice, "All of you come to me." And the crowd of boys increased under her mantle, which was ever becoming larger. Some, however, instead of seeking shelter under her mantle, ran from place to place, and they were wounded before they could find a safe shelter. The Blessed Mother continued to call out and in a louder voice, but those who ran to her became fewer. The elephant continued his attacks, and a few boys, dispersed here and there, some of them having a sword and others two swords, hindered their companions who were still in the yard from going to Mary. The elephant did not touch these at all.

Some of the boys sheltered near Mary and encouraged by her, ran out every now and then to snatch from the elephant his prey, bringing the wounded ones under the mantle of the mysterious statue. Those who were thus brought in were immediately healed. They then ran out to bring in some more. Some, armed with sticks, chased away the elephant from its victims and fought his accomplices; and they did not stop this work even at the risk of their lives, until almost all the wounded were brought to safety.

Now the yard was deserted. Some lay on the ground almost dead. On one side there was a great crowd of boys under the mantle of the Blessed Virgin; on the other side and in the distance the elephant could be seen with only those ten or twelve boys who remained with him. These were the ones who had helped him to do so much evil. And now the elephant, having raised himself on his hind legs, changed himself into a horrible specter with long horns. Then he took a big black bag and into it put those poor fellows who had helped him, ending his task by making a horrible trumpeting. Immediately a thick smoke curled all around them and they were hurled down with the monster into an abyss that opened under their feet.

When this frightful scene was over I looked around in order to manifest some of my reflections to my mother and the Professor. But I did not see them any more. I turned around to Mary to read the inscriptions embroidered on her mantle and I saw they were as follows: "He who praises me shall have life everlasting. Let the little ones come unto me. Refuge of Sinners. Salvation to those who believe in me, full of piety, meekness and mercy. Blessed are those who keep my ways."

After the disappearance of the elephant everything was calm. The Blessed Virgin seemed almost tired from calling out to the boys. After a while she addressed the boys with words of comfort and hope and having repeated those words, "He who praises me shall have life everlasting," she added, "You who listened to my words and escaped from the terrible danger had the opportunity of observing those companions of yours being thrown about and so seriously injured. Do you want to know what is the cause of their being lost? Bad language and those bad deeds that immediately follow bad talk. You have seen also those companions of yours who were brandishing a sword. They are the ones that seek your damnation, snatching you from me. They are the ones that cause the loss of so many fellow students. But those whom God suffers the longest, the more severely will He punish. That infernal demon after having enveloped them in the bag, dragged them with him to eternal damnation. And now you go in peace, but be mindful of my words. Flee from the friends of Satan. Flee from bad language and especially from language against purity. Have great confidence in me and my mantle will always be your secure refuge."

Having said these things she disappeared and there remained only the little statue in its usual place. Then my mother reappeared and again there was raised the standard with the inscription, "Holy Mary, Comforter of the Afflicted." All the boys took their place in procession behind the standard and intoned the hymn, "Praise Mary, ye faithful tongues." In a short time the singing began to die away. Then the whole scene vanished and I woke up, bathed as it were in a great perspiration.

My dear boys, you yourself can draw the conclusion. Whoever was under the mantle, whoever was thrown in the air by the elephant, and whoever was brandishing the sword, will know it by examining his conscience. I only repeat to you the words of the Blessed Virgin, "Come to me all." Have recourse to Mary. At any rate let those who were so badly treated by the brute, flee from bad language and bad companions. And those who were trying to keep the others away from Mary, let them either change their manner of life, or leave this house at once. And whoever wants to know the place he occupied let him come to my room and I will tell him.

Thus "The Elephant Dream" sermon. Anyone who has had any dealings with imaginative boys will know that such talk would be immensely effective. Whether the last invitation was accepted, we do not know. Certainly, those with guilty consciences would hardly avail themselves of that invitation, coming from the lips of one who already bore the reputation for sanctity.

Not only was Don Bosco ever interested in his Valdocco boys, but as his Oratories sprang up in other cities and other countries, from time to time he visited those he could and made more friendships. To these distant sons of his, he was a loving father. He would regularly write them. Here is a specimen of these eagerly awaited letters, that reveal the fatherliness of Don Bosco:

To my dear friends, the Director, the Community, the pupils, and to all who are at the College of Lanzo—Allow me to tell you, and none of you must take offense, that you are all thieves. I say it and I repeat it, you have taken everything. When I was at Lanzo you bewitched me by your affectionate and thoughtful regard for me; you captured all the powers of my mind by your piety; there remained to me a poor heart, of which you had stolen all its affection. Now your letter signed by two hundred most dear names has taken possession of this heart as well; in it nothing remains save a great desire to love you in our Lord, to do you some good and to save your souls. This special mark of your affection urges me to visit you as soon as possible, and I hope to come before long. On the 15th of this month, the Feast of St. Maurice, I shall say Mass for your intention; and you must do me the favor of going to Communion and praying that we may all be one day together in Heaven.

Thus ends the letter of a true father to his distant sons.

CHAPTER X

THEY WHO RETURN AT EVENING

POSSIBLY the best evidence that Don Bosco had risen to heights of sanctity is the active interest that some of the devil's own took in him. If he was not a powerful influence against Satan and all his works, Don Bosco might have gotten more sleep. Most of the material for this chapter is taken from the testimony of those older boys, who were soon to be Salesians. So we let them quote the words of Don Bosco.

The future Salesian Cardinal Cagliero has written:

> There was a real diabolical vexation, which began in the early part of February, 1862. We noticed that the health of Don Bosco was declining from day to day, and we saw that he was paler and more tired than usual. We asked him what the trouble was and if he did not feel well. Then he answered, "I need some sleep, for I have hardly shut my eyes for four or five nights."
>
> "Well, sleep," we said, "and during the night leave all your work alone."
>
> "Oh, it isn't that! I do want to sleep but someone makes me stay awake against my will."
>
> "How is that?"
>
> "For several nights past the evil spirit has amused himself with poor Don Bosco and not allowed him to sleep. You will see if he hasn't had a good time.

124

As soon as I am in bed, I hear a loud voice in my ear that stuns me and I feel a gush of wind that envelops me and scatters the papers that are on my desk and throws my books upon the floor. Some nights ago I was correcting the copy of an article, entitled 'The Power of Darkness' for the next 'Catholic Readings.' I kept the papers on my desk. On getting up in the morning I found them either on the floor or some place else in the house. The whole affair is very curious. It seems that the devil likes to stay with his friends who write about him!"

At this point Don Bosco smiled and continued: "For three nights I have been hearing someone chopping wood near my Franklin. Last night after the fire in the stove had burnt out, it rekindled itself and a terrible flame appeared, capable of burning up the whole house.

"Another time, after I had extinguished the light in the lamp, I threw myself on the bed and was just about to sleep, when, lo and behold! the covers were drawn off me in a mysterious manner, as if by a hand, and were pulled slowly toward my feet, leaving me little by little half uncovered. At first, I was willing to believe that this phenomenon was produced by a natural cause, so I took hold of the edge of the cover and started to pull it back over myself, but I had hardly arranged the covers when I felt them sliding off me again. Then, suspecting what it might be, I lit the candle, got out of bed, searched every corner of the room, but found no one and returned to go to sleep, abandoning myself to Divine Providence. While the light was lit, nothing extraordinary happened, but as soon as the candle was blown out, the covers started to move again.

"Overcome by a mysterious fright, I relit the candle and immediately that phenomenon stopped. But it began again when the room returned to darkness. One time I saw the light put out by a powerful breath. Then the pillow began to shake under my head at the very moment that I was about to fall asleep. I made the Sign of the Cross and that annoyance stopped. I recited again some prayers and composed myself, hoping to fall asleep, at least, for a few moments, but I had hardly become drowsy, when the bed was shaken by invisible hands. The door of my room started to creak and then it seemed as if it would burst open under the shock of a powerful gust of wind. I often heard about my room unusual and dreadful noises, like the rumbling wheels of carts. Now and then a very sharp cry would make me jump suddenly, and one night I saw a horrible monster open the door of my room and enter with his jaws wide open, advancing to devour me. I made the Sign of the Cross and the monster disappeared."

Don Bosco stopped and his listeners record these unusual visitations:

One night Father Angelo Savio, having resolved to watch in the antechamber of Don Bosco's room, suddenly heard a strange noise. It was toward midnight. Not being able to withstand the fear that overcame him, he fled to his own room.

Don Bosco would have liked someone to stay with him, but after Savio's account, no one had the courage to accept his invitation.

Don Bosco told of further visitations from his undesirable visitors:

> On the nights of the 6th and 7th of this month (February, 1862) I had just lain down and was beginning to fall asleep, when I felt someone take me by the shoulders and shake me so that I was greatly frightened. "Who are you?" I started to shout. I immediately lit the lamp and dressed myself. I looked under the bed and in every corner of the room to see if the one who was the cause of the trick was hidden there. But I found nobody. I examined the door of the library, but everything was closed and in order. Therefore I returned to bed. I had just fallen asleep when I felt another shake, which completely turned me over. I wanted to ring the bell to call Rossi or Reano. "But, no," I said to myself, "I do not want to disturb anyone." I lay on my back, trying to go to sleep, when I felt an enormous weight on my stomach, which prevented me from breathing. I could not help shouting, "What's that?" I struck a blow, but hit nothing. I turned around and that oppression was renewed. In such a miserable state I passed the whole night.
>
> The following night I blessed the bed before going to sleep, but it was useless, and that funny trick was continually renewed for four or five nights. To-night I will see.

On February 15 Don Bosco related the following to Mr. Oreglia, a gentleman stopping at the Oratory. "Last evening I went to my room and saw my desk dancing and beating a tattoo. 'O this is beautiful!' I said to myself and I approached and asked it: 'What do you want?' The desk tapping continued. When I would walk up and down the room it would stop, and when I would approach it, it would dance and beat time. I assure you that if I heard from some one what I am saying I would not believe it! But doesn't it seem to be the same as the facts about the witches which our grandmothers used to tell us? If I would relate such things to our boys, my goodness! they would die of fright!"

Don Bosco's listeners begged him to tell them more. At first, he did not wish to continue the discourse, replying, "When one has to say something, it is necessary to see that that account be for the glory of God and the salvation of souls."

Some of the deeply interested young clerics, who were listening in on this conversation, urged Don Bosco to go on. Finally he consented. "When I went to bed I saw at one time the form of a bear, another time, a tiger, then a wolf, then a big horrible serpent. I saw them moving around my room, climbing up on the head of the bed and staying there. I left them alone for a little while and then exclaimed: 'O Good Jesus!' Immediately, as from a blow, they all disappeared."

Cardinal Cagliero's account continues:

This evening (February 16th) some remarked that Don Bosco had not taken milk in his coffee for five or six mornings. We argued whether or not Don Bosco was doing this fasting to obtain from God relief from his nightly torments, which he had spoken about. We asked Don Bosco if he had slept well the night before and he replied: "Yes, a little."

The next morning some of us were around Don Bosco while be was taking his coffee, and asked him if he was still disturbed in the night.   He said: "The desk continued to jump and made the lampshade fall. I went to sleep, but lo! I felt a small cold brush passing over my forehead and it was moving slowly. Then I pulled my nightcap down, but that mysterious brush continued to pass over me, irritating my nose, my nostrils, and my mouth, so that I could neither sleep nor close my eyes for even a single instant. This happened other times. This morning I felt very tired."

Mr. Oreglia asked Don Bosco whether or not he was afraid when the devil annoyed him in this way.

He replied: "Horror, yes. Fear, no. Just as I have no fear of all the angels, being as I hope, a friend of God, so I have no fear of all the devils of Hell, being as I am an enemy of such enemies of God, Who will defend me. Let Satan do what he wants, now is his time, but I will have mine also."

To-day, Sunday (February 23rd), Don Bosco being very weary, was obliged to go to bed—a thing most unusual for him. . . . In the evening Father Rua went to him and asked him how he was. "I am very, very tired and unable to rest. I am continually disturbed. Last night was a continual alternation of sleeping and waking. Just as I was beginning to close my eyes, I felt a hammer banging under my pillow. I sat up on the bed and everything ceased. I lay down again and the banging began again. It was a real torment. I was wishing for the morning. When I tell these things I do so smilingly, but I assure you that I do not smile sincerely, because they give me much to think about. The past year has been an extraordinary one, but this year is still more so."

Father Rua suggested that he exorcise the evil spirit.

Don Bosco explained that he intended to use a means that he had not employed yet. Pressed for an explanation, he said, "I shall question him in the name of Jesus Christ. I will provoke him to tell me if he comes from God, Who wishes me to be subject to this trial, or from Lucifer, who intends to impede the development of this good work, which we have begun. From this he cannot escape."

Don Bosco went to spend some days with his friend, the Bishop of Ivrea, hoping that a change of residence would rid him of these nightly visitations. At first he found relief; every disturbance had ceased. One evening he had a long conversation with the Bishop up to midnight, and then went to sleep, tranquilly, thinking that the devil had lost track of him. But when the light went out, the pillow started to move under his head, as it had done at Turin. Then a horrible monster appeared at the foot of Don Bosco's bed and was about to jump on him. At the sight of such an apparition, he cried out so loudly that he awoke all those in the house. Bishop, priests and servants all rushed to Don Bosco's room at the outcry, thinking that some disaster had befallen their guest. All asked him anxiously what had happened. Don Bosco smilingly replied: "It is nothing. It is nothing. I had a dream. Don't worry. Return to bed and sleep."

The next day, however, he related everything to the Bishop.

A few days after Don Bosco had returned from Ivrea to Valdocco the disturbance recommenced. The night between March 3rd and 4th, he told some of his helpers the devil had taken the bed, raised it high, then let it fall so that his entire body was all shaken up. It seemed to him that the blood was about to burst out of his head. Said Don Bosco, "Toward morning, after the devil had disturbed me all night, one time banging the doors, another time the windows, he took the card over my desk upon which were written the words, 'Every Minute of Time Is a Treasure,' and he threw it upon the floor with such force that it seemed like the shot of a gun. Getting out of bed I found the card in the middle of the room."

Don Bosco's listeners begged him to keep the promise he had made to exorcise the devil and send him away immediately after he had returned from Ivrea.

"If I send him away from me, he will attack the boys."

Then a young priest asked him, "Then you mean to say that when you were at Ivrea and left alone by the devil for one night, he did much harm among the boys?"

"Yes; he did much harm."

They insisted that he at least ask the devil what he wished.

Don Bosco answered, "And who knows if I have not already questioned him?"

"Tell us, tell us, what he had to say?" demanded the listening group. Don Bosco turned the conversation to another question and there was no means of getting any other word from him than this, "Pray."

It was a year later that Don Bosco narrated to a group of older boys the terrible nights of those times. One who was present quotes Don Bosco thus:

One of the boys had boasted, "Oh, I am not afraid of the devil!"

"Silence," commanded the Director, in a voice that vibrated with emotion, "Silence. You do not know what power the devil has, if God would give him permission to use it."

But the boy continued, "If I should see the devil I would grab him by the neck and he would receive something from me."

"Do not talk foolishly, my dear," chided Don Bosco. "You would die from fright at the first sight of him."

"But I would make the Sign of the Cross."

"That would avail for only a moment."

"Well, Don Bosco, what did you do to get rid of him?"

"Oh, I have found the way to make him run away and not to appear for a good long while."

"And what are these means? Certainly it is the Sign of the Cross?"

"Yes; but that is not sufficient. You need something more. The Sign of the Cross is good only for the moment that it is made."

"With holy water?"

"In certain instances even holy water is not enough."

"Well, then, what is this remedy that you have used, Don Bosco?"

"I have found it and it is of great efficacy."

Don Bosco became silent and did not want to say anything else. "What is certain is that I do not wish anyone to find himself in these circumstances in which I have found myself, and it is necessary to pray to God that He prevent the devil from playing the same tricks on you."

Further than this Don Bosco would not explain. But from what we know of the lives of the Saints, we may conclude that this "remedy" had something to do with fasting and penance, neither of which, Don Bosco wisely concluded, would be practiced with discretion by his youthful listeners.

CHAPTER XI

BOYS OF GOD

ONE day a serious-looking lad dogged Don Bosco's steps in the Valdocco Oratory yard. Finally Don Bosco noticed him.

"You wish to speak with me, my son?"

"Yes, Father, I do."

With this the boy drew the priest aside and then whispered: "Father, I should like to give a present, which I hope will please you."

"What's the gift?"

"Here," said the boy, standing on tiptoe with outstretched arms and upturned face. "Here, Don Bosco, is the gift. I want to give myself to you from now on, so that you will keep me good always."

"My son," said the priest, "you could not have made a more acceptable gift. Gladly I accept you, but not for myself, but to offer and consecrate you to our dear Lord."

That lad, like other lads, never regretted his gift. For Don Bosco might have paraphrased his motto and translated it "Give me the souls of boys."

It is quite clear from what has been written that boys were the attraction in the life of Don Bosco. He loved boys and his love was returned. He liked to come to the dormitory and give his boys a short talk that would induce holy thoughts as they drifted off to sleep. One evening he said: "My dear boys, Don Bosco is the easiest man in the world to please; you may romp and shout and play and get up as many tricks as you like. He can put up with all that. But take care to do no harm to souls, as then you will find him inexorable.

"When a boy enters the Oratory my very heart is glad because I see in him a soul to be saved. When he is numbered among my children then he becomes my crown. But there are crowns of two kinds; if a boy corresponds to the care I take with him, if he makes every effort in his power to save his soul, then that boy makes my crown one of roses. But if he refuses to put my words into practice, if I see that he is careless of his soul's welfare, then I assure you he is for me a most painful crown of thorns."

A French gentleman, M. Constabile, has given us this pen picture of Don Bosco's method with his "crown of thorns":

When I went to visit Don Bosco, I found him at his desk reading a paper on which several names were written. "Here," he remarked, "are some of my little rogues, whose conduct is not satisfactory." At that time I was but imperfectly acquainted with his methods and I asked him if he had any punishment in reserve for those naughty boys.

"None at all," he replied, "but this is what I am going to do. This one, for instance (pointing to one of the names), is the worst little rascal, though he has an excellent heart. I will go to him during the time of recreation and ask about his health, and he doubtless will answer that it is excellent. 'Then you are quite satisfied with yourself,' I will say. At first he will be somewhat surprised. Then he will cast down his eyes and look ashamed. In an affectionate tone, I will insist: 'But, my child, something is wrong.

If your body is in health, perhaps your mind is not at peace. Is it long since you were at Confession?' In a few minutes the boy will be ready to confess his fault, and I am sure I shall have no more complaints of him."

Once when preaching to the Oratory boys he used this figure in speaking of his idea of discipline:

Charity must prevail in the long run. And if I am asked what is to be done when either corporal punishment or expulsion is deemed necessary, I reply that on each of the two hands with which I offer up Holy Mass I have five fingers. Now if any one were to ask me with which of them I should part, I should reply that they are all equally precious to me. But if it were judged absolutely necessary to part with one in order that I should keep the other nine, then I would consent to be deprived of that one which is least indispensable to me. Thus, first of all with the little finger, and only in extreme cases with either of these two with which I can both write and also offer up the Holy·Sacrifice. In the same way, all my children are equally dear to me, and my desire is that they all should remain at my side, and it is only when every other means has been exhausted, and delay would mean harm to the others, that I can bring myself to dismiss any one of them, and even after that, just like a man who feels the loss of a limb, Don Bosco's heart is with his son who has strayed, and he does whatever he can to save him.

This is from the sermon that later was called the "Sermon on the Fingers."

This extract shows the heart of Don Bosco. Is it any wonder that he attracted boys to him, even from his earliest days?

Among all the boys who came under Don Bosco's kindly personality there are a few boys who stand out distinguished for their remarkable sanctity. The earliest of these whose names are linked with Don Bosco was the boy, Louis Comollo. Both having similar tastes they became fast friends. Among their companions were several boys who were bullies. One afternoon these bullies were abusing Louis Comollo. John Bosco came into the room. As he himself relates the incident:

I said in a loud voice that no one should dare to touch Comollo. Some of the stronger ones accepted the challenge and one even struck Comollo. I then completely forgot myself and, not paying attention any more to reason, but using sheer brute strength, I took hold of one of these fellows, and, using him like a club, began to knock down the others. Four fell to the floor. The others took to flight, begging mercy. Just then the professor came and seeing those arms and legs swinging about and what was taking place, began to shout and rain blows on all sides. The storm was about to fall on me, but the professor asked the reason for this disorder. On learning the truth, he laughed and wished that show of strength to be repeated. Everybody laughed and no more attention was paid to the punishment I deserved.

But Comollo taught altogether different things [continues Don Bosco's narrative]. He told me God had not given me my strength in order to kill others, but that He wished us to love one another, and return good for evil.

The two pious youths became fast friends and both entered the seminary together. Comollo's health failed. John was with his friend as much as he was allowed. A pious agreement had been made between these two that the one to die first would, God willing, appear to the other. Louis Comollo died on April 2, 1839. We have Don Bosco's own account of what followed.

On the night of April 3rd, I was in the south dormitory with twenty other students. I had gone to bed, but did not sleep, for this agreement was on my mind; in fact, a sort of dread seemed to tell me that something extraordinary would happen. At midnight a heavy, mysterious noise was heard at the end of the corridor; a noise which became more ominous and terrible as it approached. It could well be likened to the noise of a heavy cart drawn by many horses, or of an express train, or to the discharge of cannon. As it approached the dormitory, it seemed to make the roof and walls and ceiling shake as though they were made of flagstones and were being struck by a powerful arm.

The noise seemed to come nearer and nearer; ever more appalling. It was now near the dormitory; it entered without the opening of doors, or rather the door was violently thrown open by unseen hands. The noise continued its terrifying course without anything making itself visible to the eye, beyond a vague light varying in color, which seemed to change with the change of sound. Of a sudden there was

silence, the light became clearer, and the voice of
Comollo was distinctly heard, "I am saved.". . .

Don Bosco added some expression on his feelings at this
fulfillment of the mutual promise. He says:

> Personally I would have preferred to die than to
> go through that frightful experience again. It was
> the first time that I remember being afraid. . . . As
> a general rule no sanction is given by Heaven to
> such compacts; but, sometimes, as in this case, God
> allows them to be fulfilled. I should never advise
> anyone to follow our example. In endeavoring to
> bring into relation with one another the natural and
> the supernatural, weak human nature suffers severely,
> particularly when there is no question of matters that
> concern our eternal salvation.

The above account was first printed in 1884, long, long
after the terrifying experience.

It was natural that among the thousands of boys who
came under Don Bosco's benign influence, there would be
some who would be inspired by their Director's holy life
and example to rise to heights of sanctity.

Don Bosco has written the biographies of three of his
saintly boys. There was Francis Besucco. Don Bosco
had called him "A Flower of Paradise." Francis's dying
words were, "I die with one regret, that I have not loved
God as He deserves to be loved!"

When death was imminent, Don Bosco was assisting
him. Other priests and boys of the Oratory were standing,
grouped around the bed. Just before Francis breathed his

last, the boy fixed his gaze in awe on something beyond the foot of the bed. All watched the dying boy. Awe changed to a most beautiful smile. And the boy started to sing one of the favorite Oratory hymns to Our Lady. The watchers, who knew Francis intimately, did not recognize this new and limpid voice. But they noticed an extraordinary brightness had filled the room. When the hymn was finished, Francis lay back on the pillow. Don Bosco approached and found that the boy was dead. Surely "A Flower of Paradise!"

Then there was Michael Magone. Don Bosco describes his first meeting with this anything but over holy small boy:

One evening in autumn [says Don Bosco in the biography] I had to wait an hour at Carmagnola for the train, and the gloom prevented my seeing beyond a step. The dull lamps of the station emitted but faint light, whilst the street lamps were lost in obscurity. The darkness did not, however, stop the romping diversions of a troop of children, whose noise deafened the bystanders. Loud shouts of "Wait. Run. Take that. Stop him. That fellow will escape!" completely put an end to any conversation among the waiting passengers. In the midst of the turmoil a clear distinct voice was heard, in a commanding tone, as if from a leader. The orders were echoed here and there, almost instantly obeyed, and quietness ensued. I felt a strong wish to know whose was the power that so promptly and authoritatively brought order out of chaos, and I quickly went among the boys who were congregated around their chief. They ran away frightened, only one remained, who turned toward me, his hands on his hips, evidently ready to fight.

"Who are you, and why do you interrupt our play?"

"A friend," I said.

"What do you want?"

"To join you, if you will allow me."

"But who are you? I do not know you."

"I repeat, a friend, anxious to join you and your friends. Who are you?"

"I," the small boy said in a grave tone, "I am Michael Magone, general of recreation."

During this dialogue the rest of the children who had dispersed in a panic, returned one by one and formed a circle round us. After a few trivial remarks to them, I again spoke to Magone.

"My dear Magone, how old are you?"

"Thirteen years."

"Have you been to Confession?"

"Yes, yes," and he burst out laughing.

"Have you made your First Communion?"

"Yes."

"Have you learnt any occupation?"

"Yes—idling."

"Is your father alive?"

"No, my father is dead."

"And your mother?"

"My mother works and earns what she can to support my brothers and me, who perpetually worry her."

Don Bosco was won by this candor. So he asked him, "Would you like to learn a trade or study?"

Michael Magone uttered the Italian equivalent for "Sure, Father."

Don Bosco's train was coming into the station so he gave the boy a medal of Our Lady, Help of Christians, saying, "Take this to the priest of this parish, and he will tell you about me."

With this the first meeting terminated. The boy's curiosity to learn more of this attractive priest, sent him at once to the parish priest. Shortly thereafter Don Bosco brought this promising boy to the Oratory of St. Francis of Sales. He told Michael, "I shall admit you, but only on the condition that you do not turn this house upside down."

"I shall not give you any trouble, Father. Try me," promised Michael. And he kept his promise.

Later, Don Bosco asked him what he would like to become. Michael hesitated and replied, "If a good-for-nothing like me could ever become good enough to become a priest like you, I would like to be one some day."

The life at the Oratory was different from the street life Michael had been accustomed to. Don Bosco describes its gradual effect on this boy.

> He became very sad. He never smiled. Often during recreation he retired to a quiet corner to reflect and at times to cry. I observed him closely and at an opportune moment called him: "My dear Magone, I wish you to grant me a favor, but I do not like to be refused."
>
> "Only speak, Father. There is nothing that I would not do for you."
>
> "I wish that for one moment you would allow me to be master of your thoughts. Yes! Open your heart to me, my poor child, that I may know the cause of your sorrow."

This kindness touched Michael. He burst out, "O, Father, I am in despair!"

He cried bitterly. I waited until he became calmer, and then said in a tone of pleasantry. "Is this the General Michael Magone, chief of the band at Carmagnola! What a general! You who could command so well, cannot find words to express your feelings!"

"I do not know how."

"Tell me one word."

"My conscience is troubling me all the time."

"Enough, my child, I understand. Now that you have said these few words, I can say the rest."

And with all the gentleness that Don Bosco was master of, he led the little fellow to make a general confession.

After that the sun shone continuously in Michael's countenance.

Don Bosco gives us a further light on the growth to holiness of this impetuous soul:

I took him with others, for the vacation at Becchi. One day all went to amuse themselves in the woods. Some gathered mushrooms, others shook chestnuts from the laden trees, or piled up gigantic heaps of leaves. Magone quietly disappeared; a comrade perceived and followed him, fearing he was ill. Michael, believing himself unnoticed, returned to the house, and went to the chapel, where, kneeling before the Blessed Sacrament, he remained absorbed in prayer until the voices of his returning comrades disturbed him. Interrogated later as to why he thus isolated himself, he replied: "Because I feared to fall again into sin, so I went to beg Jesus in His Sacrament to give me strength and perseverance."

On another occasion Don Bosco heard crying at night in the dormitory. He investigated and found Michael. "Are you ill, my child?" he asked.

Michael became confused and blushed, but when the Director repeated the question he answered in these words. "I am thinking about the moon, Father, that for so many centuries shines regularly in the sky, obedient to the order of our Creator, while I, a rational being, have frequently, though young, disobeyed and in a thousand ways offended God." Don Bosco consoled the boy, wondering at the tender conscience of this youth scarcely fourteen years of age.

Michael Magone did not live much longer. Don Bosco has written this account of his death:

Suddenly Michael called, "Father, do not leave me."

"Be sure," said I, "I shall not leave you until you are with our Savior in Heaven; but as you are going to leave this world, would you not like to say farewell to your mother?"

"No, I do not like to give her such pain."

"Well, at least you will send her a message?"

"Yes; ask her to pardon all the sorrow and trouble I caused her during my life; tell her I repent bitterly, that I love her very much. She must be brave, and I shall wait for her in Heaven."

At these words, those present could not refrain from tears. Don Bosco asked the boy a few questions to occupy his dying moments with good thoughts.

"What shall I say to your comrades?"

"Always to make good Confessions."

"Of the actions of your life, what gives you now most pleasure?"

"The remembrance of even the little I have done in honor of the Blessed Virgin. Oh! Mary, Mother of God, how happy it is to die your servant! Nevertheless, Father, one thought troubles me. When my soul separates from my body, and enters the Eternal Kingdom, what shall I do?"

"Do not fear," I said. "The Blessed Virgin will accompany you before the Sovereign Judge. Leave all to her. But before you go I wish to give you a message."

"Ready, Father."

"When you see the Blessed Mother of our Savior in Paradise, present humble, respectful greetings from me and all here. Ask her to bless and take us under her powerful protection, that not one of us, nor those whom Providence will send to our Oratories, may be lost."

"I will, Father. Is that all?"

"Yes, for the present. Now, my son, rest yourself."

Shortly afterwards little Michael set off obediently on his long journey to deliver Don Bosco's message to the Lady All Fair. It takes the faith of saints to send such messages by such messengers.

Of all the boys who came under Don Bosco's influence the holiest was Dominic Savio. The Cause of this fifteen-year-old boy was introduced for Beatification and Canonization on February 11, 1914, and he is now a Saint.

Dominic was born April 2, 1842, at Riva di Chieri,

near Turin. At seven he received his First Holy Communion and made these resolutions:

1. I will go to Confession often and as frequently to Holy Communion as my confessor allows.
2. I wish to sanctify the Sundays and festivals in a special manner.
3. My friends shall be Jesus and Mary.
4. Death rather than sin.

These four resolutions beautifully sum up his brief life. At ten a gentleman met Dominic on a country road, trudging along under the broiling sun.

"Are you not afraid to go so far alone?"

"I am not alone," replied Dominic gravely. "I have my Angel Guardian with me, accompanying every step."

"But surely you find the journey long and tiresome in this very hot weather?"

"Nothing seems tiresome or painful when you are working for a master who pays well."

"And who is your master?"

"It is God, our Creator, Who rewards even a cup of cold water given for love of Him."

If these were the thoughts of little Dominic at ten, they show he was already a long way on the road to sanctity. Don Bosco tells of his first meeting with the holiest of his small charges:

> I questioned him about his studies and his desires for the future, and we were immediately on the most friendly and confidential terms. I may say that I at once recognized a boy after God's own heart, and I could not help being struck by the workings of grace, already manifest in one of such tender years.

Don Bosco spoke of Dominic's coming to the Oratory: "And what do you think you can make of me, Father?" "Something beautiful and acceptable to God."

Thus was the compact made and the sequel shows how well the material turned out. This is not the place to go into the life of this last century edition of St. Stanislaus, but a few incidents in his life may be mentioned:

Very often [writes Don Bosco] when Dominic went into the church, principally on his Communion days, or when the Blessed Sacrament was exposed, he fell into what was clearly a sort of rapture or ecstasy; and thus he would remain for a very long time, if he were not called away to fulfill his ordinary tasks.

It happened one day that he was absent from breakfast, from class, from the mid-day meal, and no one knew where he was. He was not in the study, nor in the dormitory. The Director [Don Bosco himself] was informed and he had a suspicion that he knew where to find him. He went to the church, and up into the choir near the sanctuary. There stood the boy like a statue; one foot was in front of the other, and one hand was on a bookstand near-by, while the other was on his breast. His face was turned toward the sanctuary and his gaze was fixed on the tabernacle. His lips were not moving. The Director called him; no reply; he shook him gently; then Dominic turned and said: "Oh, is the Mass over?" "See," said the priest, showing him his watch, "it is two o'clock." The boy said he was sorry for the transgression of the rule, and the Director sent him off to dinner, saying: "If anyone asks you where you have been, say that you have been carrying out an order of mine."

Dominic, when questioned by Don Bosco, as to what had happened when he stayed behind on this occasion, answered simply: "I became distracted, and losing the thread of my prayers, I beheld such beautiful and entrancing sights that hours seem to go in a moment."

There was another occasion when Dominic took the priest to a soul in cruel need.

As Don Bosco tells it:

> One day Dominic came to my room and said: "Come quickly, Father, come with me, there is a good work to be done."
>
> "Where am I to go?" I asked. "Make haste, make haste," he said. I hesitated, but as he insisted, and past experience had shown me the importance of such invitations, I went down with him. He went first, I followed. Down one street, then another, then a third, all in silence; there was yet another turning, and at a certain door he stopped; there he went up the stairs to the third floor, rang the bell vigorously, and turning to me said: "It is here that you are wanted." Then he went away.
>
> The door was opened and a woman appeared. "Oh, make haste," she said. "Quick, or it will be too late! My husband has abandoned his faith; now he is at the point of death and wishes to die a Catholic."

Don Bosco brought peace to the man. Later, Don Bosco asked Dominic how he knew that there was a man ill at that house. He did not answer, but looked at him with an air of sadness, and Don Bosco noticed that tears were beginning to come, so he did not question him further.

This boy of God wished to see the Pope, Pius IX, as he had something of importance to tell him. He repeated this desire on various occasions. Once Don Bosco asked him what this important matter was.

Dominic replied: "If I could have an interview with the Pope, I would tell him, that in spite of the great tribulations which he has to endure at present, he should never slacken in his particular solicitude for England. God is preparing a great triumph for Catholicism in that kingdom."

"Why, what grounds have you for that statement?" inquired Don Bosco.

"I will tell you, but do not mention it to others, for they might think it ridiculous. But if you go to Rome, tell Pius IX for me. This is why I think so. One morning, during my Thanksgiving after Communion, I had a distraction, which was strange for me; I thought I saw a great stretch of country enveloped in a thick mist, and it was filled with a multitude of people. They were moving about, but like men, who, having missed their way, are not sure of their footing. Somebody near by said: 'This is England.' I was going to ask some questions about it when I saw His Holiness, Pius IX, as I had seen him represented in pictures. He was majestically clad, and was carrying a shining torch with which he approached the multitude as if to enlighten their darkness. As he drew near, the light of the torch seemed to disperse the fog, and the people were left in broad daylight. 'This torch,' said my informant, 'is the Catholic religion which is to illuminate England.'"

When Don Bosco went to Rome in 1858 he related this

to the Holy Father, who was greatly interested and said: "What you have told me confirms me in my resolution to do all that is possible for England, which has long been the object of my special care. What you have related is, to put it at its lowest estimation, the counsel of a devout soul."

It was Pius IX who reëstablished the Catholic Hierarchy in England.

Dominic Savio died in his fifteenth year. This description of his death is taken from Don Bosco's "Life of Dominic Savio":

By the evening of March 9th, he had received all the consolations of our Holy Religion. Anyone listening to his voice, or noticing his cheerful countenance would have thought he was lying in bed for a little rest. His bright manner, his looks, still full of life, the complete possession of his senses, quite astonished everyone, and nobody, except himself, believed Dominic to be at the point of death.

An hour and a half before he passed away, the parish priest came to see him, and seeing how calm he was, he was surprised to hear him recommending his soul to God. He continued to make aspirations and short ejaculations expressing his desire to go speedily to Heaven. The priest remarked, "Oh! I am at a loss to know what to suggest for the recommendation of a soul of this sort."

He recited some prayers, and was about to leave, when Dominic asked him for some final thought by way of remembrance. The priest said he could recommend nothing to him but the thought of the

Sacred Passion; Dominic thanked him for this and continued to recall it, and to repeat invocations to Jesus and Mary. Then he rested for about half an hour.

At the end of that time he turned to his parents and said, "It is time."

The father replied: "I am here, my son, what would you like?"

"It is time, Father; get my prayer book, and read the prayers for a good death."

At these words the mother began to weep, and had to go out of the room. The father was greatly moved, but he restrained his grief so as to read the prayers. Dominic repeated them after him, and, in the proper place, said: "Merciful Jesus, have mercy on me."

When they came to the part which says: "But deign to receive me into Thy Kingdom where I may forever sing Thy praises," Dominic added: "Yes; that is exactly what I desire; to sing the praises of God for all eternity."

He now seemed to rest a moment, as though pondering over something in his mind. Then he opened his eyes again, and said with a clear voice and a smiling countenance: "Good-by, Father, good-by; the priest wanted to tell me something else, but I cannot remember it now . . . Oh! what a beautiful sight I behold!" Thus speaking, with his hands joined, and a smile on his lips, his soul passed away.

It was March 9, 1857, and when Dominic was within a month of his fifteenth birthday.

These are brief stories from the lives of some of the boys of God who rose to heights of sanctity while under the care of Don Bosco. He was their model and they copied him accurately.

CHAPTER XII

DON BOSCO, FINANCIER

THE Founder of the Salesians was called upon to feed and clothe armies of boys and erect many buildings for their housing during his busy lifetime. Naturally we are interested in his methods of raising funds. If we could only adopt them, most of our financial difficulties in life would vanish.

One day, Don Bosco, questioned by some gentlemen of finance, as to his marvelously successful way of raising the money he needed to execute his plans, gave this explanation. One of the gentlemen had said to the holy financier: "Father, how do you manage to cover all those expenses for your Oratory, and for so many other houses? It seems quite a secret, or I should say, a mystery."

"Oh, I am always going like a steam engine," explained Don Bosco simply.

"I don't quite understand. How do you keep the engine going?"

"It must have plenty of fire inside and something to feed the fire."

"Yes. Yes. I quite understand the necessity of that, but to what fire do you refer?"

"The fire of faith and confidence in Almighty God. And without these," Don Bosco concluded, "empires fall, kingdoms are shattered, and the work of man is useless."

There is Don Bosco's explanation of "always going like a steam engine" in matters financial. Let us come down to some examples.

You remember, back in the early days of the Valdocco Oratory, Don Bosco rented the Pinardi house and grounds. It soon became evident that he would have to purchase the site and the building if he was to have anything permanent. There was one big difficulty in the way of the purchase. Signor Pinardi held his property in high estimation. Thus the real estate deal hung fire for many months. Finally in February, 1851, Signor Pinardi approached his tenant, standing in front of the church. "Oh, Don Bosco," he said, "when do you intend to purchase my house?"

"Well, as soon as ever Signor Pinardi is willing to sell it to me for what it is worth."

"That I am quite ready to do."

"What is your price then?"

"Sixteen thousand dollars."

"We had better drop the matter at once, as that is impossible."

"Well, what will you offer?"

"I do not feel inclined to make any offer."

"Why not?"

"Because what you ask is an exorbitant price; and my offer may give offence."

"No. No. You could not offend me, Don Bosco. Make your offer."

"Very well. The other day I had the place estimated by a builder—a friend of yours and mine—and he declared that the property in its present condition is worth between fifty-two hundred and fifty-six hundred dollars. I am willing to offer you six thousand dollars."

Don Bosco was more than astonished when Pinardi

replied: "Add one hundred dollars as a present for my wife and pay cash?"

"Yes," immediately replied the priest.

"When will you settle the account?"

"Whenever you choose, Signor."

"Then settle for the property two weeks from to-morrow."

Don Bosco agreed. There was only one difficulty. He did not have sixty-one hundred dollars; only a small fraction of that sum on hand. So he retired to the chapel to pray with full confidence to Our Lady, Help of Christians. That afternoon a priest, Father Cafasso, who was interested in this boy work, called at the Oratory. "Father John, I am here to give you news which, I am sure, will please you. A kind lady has entrusted me with two thousand dollars which I am to hand over to you to be used as you think best, for the greater glory of God."

"Praise to God and His Holy Mother!" replied Don Bosco. "This is certainly providential."

The next day a Rosminian Father came to the Oratory. He had a trust fund of four thousand dollars, and he thought he would consult Don Bosco as to the best way of investing it.

"God has certainly sent you to me," stated Don Bosco, and he offered to pay a fair yearly interest on the sum. The Rosminian Father agreed.

Thus, within twenty-four hours, six thousand dollars had come. The remaining one hundred dollars was given by the banker, who arranged the transfer of the property. And so Pinardi's property passed into the possession of Don Bosco.

A day came when there was not enough money in the Oratory treasury to pay the baker for the boys' daily bread.   The long-suffering baker sent notice that no more bread would be delivered until payment was made. Shortly after this ultimatum arrived, a certain count called at the Oratory, begging Don Bosco's prayers for his sick wife.   They were promised.   In leaving, the count handed Don Bosco some bank notes.   They were just half the sum due the baker.   The money was soon on its way to the bakery and bread was delivered.

Three days later, the count returned to the Oratory.   "I owe you a thousand thanks, Don Bosco," said the count.

"Rather, it is I who have to thank you," was the priest's reply.

But the count would not hear of such a thing.   His wife had that morning been pronounced out of danger and as a slight return to God and Don Bosco, the count duplicated the sum he had given on his former visit.   Don Bosco calmly accepted the offering and within the hour it was in the baker's safe and the daily bread supply was saved till the next time of financial stringency.

The Oratory building proving inadequate, Don Bosco decided, after prayer, he had to build a new wing, extending from the central gateway to the Church of St. Francis of Sales.   So he sent for Juvenal Delponte, an architect and contractor.   "Have you any money to start building, Juvenal?"

"No, Don Bosco."

"Neither have I."

"Then what shall we do?"

"Let us make a start, my friend, and before the time comes to pay the workmen, Our Lady, Help of Christians, will send us some money."

The contractor set to work.   Don Bosco retired to his chapel, and as usual, benefactors came with unclasped pocketbooks. Don Bosco took what he needed and the wing was paid for when it opened.

In 1860 Don Bosco had five hundred boys on his hands. He needed the adjoining house. Father Vaschetti, one of the Oratory boys of those days, tells the financing of this purchase:

> We were keeping the feast of St. Augustine, the patron of our dormitory, and we had every reason to be happy, because Don Bosco had come to speak to us and give us his blessing. In the meanwhile a gentleman arrived, somewhat advanced in years, but still very active. As there were no chairs about, Don Bosco had taken a seat upon a trunk, and the gentleman, whom I did not know, did the same. Turning to Don Bosco, he said, "I hear that you have bought the house next door. I am very glad to hear it. But how will you manage to pay for it?"
>
> "That," explained Don Bosco, "is a secret of Divine Providence. It requires sixteen thousand dollars."
>
> "Well, then," said the old gentleman, "you may depend on me for eight thousand dollars. Come to my house to-morrow and I will give it to you."
>
> "I gazed at the man who spoke of thousands of dollars as we would of a cent, and in my heart I thanked God for consoling Don Bosco, who was unable to hide his gratitude. All this was settled while the two were seated upon the old trunk in our dormitory.

It is not recorded where the other eight thousand dollars came from. But, no doubt, Divine Providence furnished it on time.

Don Bosco has himself told us how he viewed financial difficulties:

> God is in Israel [he would exclaim]! Let nothing disturb us!

> He would add: If I cannot remove difficulties, I do as the man does who meets an obstacle in his path; he climbs over it or finds a way around. Or, if it would mean useless loss of time, I leave one work and begin another, without losing sight of the first, for the obstacle usually dwindles in time.

He had perfect confidence that any debts he contracted for his boy work would be paid by Divine Providence, Whose Banker was usually Our Lady.

Mary, Help of Christians, proved such a benefactor of Don Bosco's various works that he decided in 1862 that she should be rewarded by having a Basilica built in her honor under that title. The financing of this Basilica is one of the romances of the Oratory. Don Bosco was so poor at the time that he did not have money enough to buy stamps to send out letters to his Salesian Coöperators.

Some prudent Salesians objected.

"Begin the work," commanded Don Bosco, and added a truism, "When did we ever begin anything with the money already in hand!"

This argument silenced opposition and the immense Basilica of Our Lady, Help of Christians, was started. Shortly afterwards Don Bosco was called to visit a lady who had been bedridden for over three months.

She opened the conversation: "O Don Bosco, if I could only get back a little health, I would say any amount of prayers, or make any sacrifice; it would be a tremendous relief if I could only get out of bed."

"Then, madam, make a Novena to Our Lady, Help of Christians," suggested the priest.

"And what must I say?"

"For nine days recite three times daily the Our Father, Hail Mary, and 'Glory Be to the Most Holy Sacrament,' and three times the 'Hail, Holy Queen' to our Blessed Lady."

"I shall do that gladly, and what work of charity shall I perform?"

"If you agree, and if you obtain some clear improvement in your health, you will make an offering for the Church of Our Lady, Help of Christians, which is just begun at Valdocco."

"I am quite willing to do that; and if during this Novena I obtain the favor of only being able to get up and go about my room, I shall make an offering toward the church of which you speak."

On the last day of the Novena Don Bosco needed two hundred dollars to pay an immediate building bill. He therefore went again to call on this bedridden lady. The maid told Don Bosco that her mistress was so perfectly cured that she had been out of the house several times. Then the lady came into the parlor.

"Oh, Don Bosco, I am cured! I have already been to thank Our Lady, and, see, here is the offering I promised to make. It is the first, but it shall not be the last."

She handed Don Bosco an envelope. When he returned to the Oratory, he found that it contained the two hundred dollars he needed. So that bill was paid.

On another occasion at this time Don Bosco called on Baron Cotta, a Senator, whom he found very ill.

"Don Bosco, I am dying," said the baron.

"What would you do if Our Lady, Help of Christians, obtained your cure from God?"

"Do? I would subscribe four hundred dollars a month for six months to your new church."

Don Bosco smiled. "Very well, Senator, I will return at once to the Oratory, where I shall get everyone to pray to Our Lady in your behalf. So cheer up."

A few days later a rejuvenated Baron Cotta called at the Oratory with the first four hundred dollars.

Doctor D'Espiney is authority for the following contribution:

On November 16, 1866, Don Bosco had not a cent in his strong box. He needed eight hundred dollars by nightfall for the new church. From early morning Father Rua, prefect of the Oratory of St. Francis of Sales, and some others, had been in the country collecting, and at eleven o'clock returned with the sum of two hundred dollars. They told Don Bosco that they firmly believed that any further begging would be a useless waste of time. As they finished the account of their unsuccessful begging journey they looked at Don Bosco with an expression of dismay. He observed gaily: "The dinner hour has struck. After dinner serious business." They followed him to the refectory. An hour later he took his hat and his beads and went toward the New Gate. He went by chance, or rather guided by Providence. A liveried servant, who was at the door of a handsome house, stopped the priest and asked him to visit his master. Don Bosco did not know the house. He entered and was ushered into the presence of a middle-aged man in bed, and evidently a sad sufferer.

"Ah, Father, you ought to cure me."

"I wish I could. Have you been ill long?"

"I have been in bed three years. I cannot stir, and the physicians give no hope. Ah! if you will lessen my sufferings your works will gain."

"Really? That will suit admirably. My works are in urgent need this evening of six hundred dollars.

The invalid exclaimed: "If it were only sixty dollars. But six hundred dollars!"

"Let us not speak of it again," said Don Bosco. And after some trivial remarks he arose to leave the room.

"Father, my cure?"

"My dear sir, I have not the power. God alone can cure you—but when you bargain with Him . . ."

"But, Father, six hundred dollars!"

"I do not insist." Don Bosco got up again to depart.

"At all events, Father, obtain some relief for me, and before the end of the year I will try to get together six hundred dollars."

"At the end of the year! But I need that sum to-night!"

"This evening? I have no money in the house. I shall have to send to the bank."

"Go yourself," ordered Don Bosco.

"You are joking, Father. Have I not told you I have been lying here three years?"

"Nothing is impossible with God. Let us appeal to the intercession of Mary, Help of Christians."

Don Bosco called in all the household, numbering some thirty, and recited the Novena prayers in which the wondering household joined. Then he ordered the servants to dress their master. They exclaimed: "Dress the master! It is three years since he was up and we do not know where to find his clothes!"

"Go buy some at once," ordered the invalid imperiously. "The Father must be obeyed."

The gentleman's doctor came in at this time and told him he was insane in attempting to walk. The clothes were quickly purchased, the patient was dressed, and to the inexpressible astonishment of the doctor and all present, the man walked across this room. He ordered his carriage and while awaiting it, called for some refreshments. This was another shock to the household, as their master had had no appetite for a long while. He descended to the carriage unassisted, and drove to his bank. Don Bosco waited at the gentleman's house, till he returned with the six hundred dollars. He kept repeating again and again, "I am quite cured and I owe it all to you, Father."

Don Bosco shook his head, and corrected the gentleman: "No, Our Blessed Lady, Help of Christians, enabled you to draw out the sum she needed from the bank to pay one of her bills."

Thus with Mary, rather actively engaged in furnishing her favorite son with the money needed, the Basilica took shape. When it was solemnly dedicated on June 19, 1868, it had cost about two hundred and twenty thousand dollars. Of this amount over one hundred and seventy thousand dollars were given in thanksgiving for favors received. Don Bosco was well within the bounds of truth when he used to say that Our Lady had financed her own church.

To cover his own remarkable power Don Bosco always had the grateful recipients of his cures and favors direct their thanks to Our Lady, Help of Christians. This confidence in Divine Providence and Our Lady never forsook Don Bosco. Through his remaining years he was accustomed to go ahead with what he thought was God's work —Our Lady's work. And when the money was needed, the money came.

Years later, there was a remarkable manifestation of this continuous power. One day, the Director of a Salesian House arrived at Turin and asked Don Bosco for a certain sum to pay an urgent debt. Don Bosco told the Prefect to give him all the money in the house, but it fell short of the amount required by exactly three hundred and ninety-two dollars. Director and Prefect therefore went to Don Bosco, who said: "You are hard to please! I gave all to the Prefect a short time ago, but since then something else may have come in."

Don Bosco went to a drawer, where he kept contributions given him for his works, and scooping up all the money there, told the other two Salesian Fathers to count it. They did and their astonishment may be imagined when it totalled up to exactly three hundred and ninety-two dollars. Don Bosco, unique financier!

CHAPTER XIII

THE MAN OF MANY WORKS

A SIDE of Don Bosco's work that has hardly been mentioned is his writing. During the period between 1845 and 1860 he published most of his works. The wonder grows how this zealous laborer of the Lord ever found time in the midst of his many distracting occupations to write one book; much less the seventy books and pamphlets that bear his name. Reading a list of his works is like walking through a well-stocked library and glancing at several titles in each section. For instance, *The Month of Mary, Arithmetic Made Easy, Life of Dominic Savio, Instructions to Young Men in the Practice of Their Duties, The Fortune House,* a play for boys, and *The History of Italy.* This latter became a standard work and has gone through twenty-six editions. Besides these, he wrote and published at regular intervals *Catholic Readings,* a magazine that deals popularly with religious topics of the day. This was the forerunner of the world-wide *Salesian Bulletin.*

Don Bosco, as an author, deliberately chose a popular style, simple, direct, and appealing to the ninety-five rather than the more highly educated five. There is a manly piety apparent on Don Bosco's pages, a reflection of that practical spirituality that was second nature to him. As the Salesian Society spread beyond Turin and the borders of Italy and of Europe, the writings of its saintly Founder were translated into other languages and renewed their good influence. Only God and the Guardian Angels know the good these religious-toned books and pamphlets did and are doing. Don Bosco, a Catholic author, is still exerting his wholesome influence in far-flung quarters in our own days.

The original Oratories at Turin had been duplicated in other Italian cities and there were gradually growing up around Don Bosco his spiritual sons, trained in his spirit and anxious to carry forward boy work along the lines of their Founder. The vast majority of these pioneer Salesians were former Oratory boys, now seminarians and earnest young priests. Don Bosco's Society had received Papal approbation in 1874, and he was the natural choice for Superior General.

Dealing with poorer boys in the various cities Don Bosco often encountered the problem of the destitute sister of the boy. Divine Providence had organized a sisterhood, under the pious Mary Mazzarello. These sisters gradually developed into the Congregation of Mary, Help of Christians. Working with Don Bosco they took up the girl work that corresponded to his Oratory work, and this Congregation became the Salesian Sisters.

Another gradual foundation was that of the Salesian Coöperators. This became the Third Order of St. Francis of Sales. It was, and is, composed of men and women in the world, who wished to further Don Bosco's work among the young. Like the other foundation of Don Bosco it had its humble start in the voluntary services of certain Turin women, who, desiring to help Mama Margaret in her household work, offered to come at regular times to Valdocco and attend to the multitudinous washings and mendings which the clothes of Don Bosco's lively charges needed. A simple rule was drawn up by

Don Bosco and revised and changed as experience showed
a better rule. The duties of Coöperators are to help destitute children by furthering Salesian works, either by a
monthly or annual offering, or in collecting and receiving
gifts and alms for the same purpose. The rules of this
Third Order of Don Bosco were submitted to Pius IX in
1874. His Holiness promptly approved of it and enriched
it with many indulgences.

Mention has been made of some of the remarkable
dreams that influenced Don Bosco's decisions. Among
the most notable is the one Don Bosco had in 1874. Several years later he related it as follows:

> It seemed to me that I was in a wild region, a
> region altogether unknown to me. It was an immense
> plain, all uncultivated, in which neither hills nor
> mountains were seen. However, in its very far
> extremity steep mountains formed one side. On the
> plain, I saw a crowd of men. They were almost
> naked, of extraordinary height and size, of ferocious
> aspect, with rough long hair of a brown and blackish
> color, and dressed only in long mantles of skins of
> animals, which hung down from their backs. They
> had for weapons a kind of long spear and a sling.
>
> These crowds of men, scattered here and there,
> offered to the spectators diverse scenes. These were
> running, hunting after wild animals; those were
> walking and carrying, stuck to the points of their
> spears, pieces of fresh meat. Here some fought
> among themselves; others fought with soldiers
> dressed in the European style and the ground was
> covered with corpses. I was trembling on seeing this
> spectacle. Suddenly, at the extremity of the plain, I

see many personages burst forth, whom, from their
dress and way of acting, I recognized as missionaries
of different Orders. They drew near in order to
preach to those barbarians the religion of Jesus Christ.
I looked at them very attentively, but I did not know
anyone. They went into the midst of those savages,
but the barbarians as soon as they saw the missionaries, with devilish fury and joy attacked them.
Ferociously they slaughter and cut the missionaries
to pieces and fasten the pieces on the points of their
long spears. Then, from time to time, the savages
fight among themselves and with the neighboring
people. After having seen such horrible slaughters,
I said to myself, "How can this people, so brutal, be
converted?" And I see in the distance a band of
other missionaries, who approached the savages with
cheerful countenances and who were preceded by
a legion of young boys.

I trembled on thinking, "They come only to be
killed!" And I went close to them. They were
seminarians and priests. I recognized them to be our
own Salesians. Those in front were known to me,
and although I could not have known personally
many others who followed the first ones, I perceived
that they were also our own Salesians.

"How in the world is this?" I exclaimed. I did
not like them to go ahead, and I was about to stop
them right there. I expected every moment that they
would experience the same fate as the older missionaries. I wanted to make them turn back, when I saw
that their appearance made joyful all those crowds
of barbarians. They lowered their weapons, put off
their ferocious expressions, and received our mission-

aries with every sign of courtesy. Astonished at this, I said to myself, "Let us see how this is going to end!" And I saw that our missionaries advanced toward those hordes of savages, instructed them, and they learned quickly; admonished them, and they accepted and put into practice their admonitions.

I stood there in order to observe and noticed that the missionaries recited the Holy Rosary, while more savages, running from every side, with one accord answered that prayer.

After a while the Salesians placed themselves in the center of the throng, which surrounded them, and there they knelt down. The savages, having put down their weapons on the ground also, bent their knees. And see! One of those Salesians intones, "Praise ye, Mary, O tongues of the Faithful!" And those crowds, all with one voice, continued the melody of this song of praise in such unison and with so much power, that I awoke.

I had that dream four or five years ago and it made a great impression on my soul. Yet, I did not understand fully its particular meaning. I understood, however, that there was question of the foreign missions, which before now had formed my most lively desire.

This prophetic dream kept urging Don Bosco. Like all true-hearted founders, he longed to send the sons and daughters of his young foundations into distant horizons to extend the Kingdom of God. The opportunity came from an unexpected source. An Oratory had been established at Varazze. When Don Bosco visited his new school the Consul of the Argentine Republic came to see him. He disclosed that as he had made his fortune in the Argentine he was anxious to do good for that country. And so he had approached the Archbishop of Buenos Aires, begging him to invite Don Bosco to send Salesians out there and into Patagonia. Don Bosco listened eagerly. He promised the Consul he would give a final decision when he had seen Pius IX.

Shortly after, Don Bosco went to Rome and His Holiness gave his heartiest approval to the plan of sending Salesians to South America. The first Salesian missioners, ten priests and brothers, and fifteen sisters, left in November, 1875. Don Bosco concluded his farewell sermon with these words: "Go, my dear sons and daughters in St. Francis of Sales, with the blessing of the Successor of St. Peter, head of the Apostles; with the blessing of our venerable Archbishop; allow my feeble hands also to bless you once more. Salesians, do not forget the family from which you are about to be separated, and your father who received you into it, whose hearts will follow you."

Don Bosco entrusted the leadership of this, his first missionary venture, to Father Cagliero. And well he could, for this was a beloved son, who had come to the Oratory as a lad of thirteen and died a Salesian Cardinal. That Don Bosco knew something of the high ecclesiastical future of this boy is clear from some remarkable incidents. One day Don Bosco joined a group of Oratory boys and said smilingly: "Let us prophecy." All looked at their Director in expectant silence. Don Bosco was silent for a moment and then he spoke. "One of you will be a Bishop." The boys looked to see at which one of them Don Bosco was looking, but he kept his eyes downcast. However, in 1854, when John Cagliero was sixteen he became so seriously sick that hope of his recovery was abandoned. Don Bosco entered the room of the dying boy and beheld a dove flying about the room with an olive branch in its beak. He saw the dove fly over the bed and drop the branch on the forehead of the boy. Don Bosco came nearer the bed to see better, and then he noticed a number of horrible phantoms grouped around the head of the bed. Looking more attentively, Don Bosco made out two human faces that stood out more prominently. One was bronze-skinned and hideous; the other, had the features of a dignified warrior. Don Bosco noticed that these two were gazing anxiously into the face of the dying boy as if hoping to discover something in his countenance.

Don Bosco gazed at the vision and then stooping over the pillow, he said: "John, my son, which do you prefer; to go to Heaven or to recover?"

Cagliero looked up into his Director's kindly face and exclaimed: "Whatever Don Bosco wishes."

"Then, my dear son, you will not die now. You will recover to be a priest and a missionary. You will travel far and work hard for the salvation of Our Master's souls."

This prophecy was a secret between the boy and his spiritual father till after Don Bosco's death in 1888, when John Cagliero was a Bishop and related what his Founder had told him.

That first band of Salesian missioners settled at San Nicholas in the Argentine. Like all pioneer missioners they met with seemingly unsurmountable difficulties, and like their predecessors in other fields afar, they overcame these difficulties. In 1879 they penetrated into Patagonia, to bring the Kingdom of God into that bleak, godless strip at the southern tip of South America. When they sent pictures of their converts back to Turin, Don Bosco recognized them as the savages of his dream.

Yearly, Salesian sons and daughters were dispatched by Don Bosco into these beloved South American fields. And the story of their remarkable growth is one of the nineteenth-century triumphs of the Church Missionary.

CHAPTER XIV

THE WONDER-WORKER OF TURIN

SPREAD throughout the busy days of Don Bosco, like pearls on a string, are some remarkable happenings that were not passed over in silence by those who experienced them or heard them. Don Bosco had a reputation as a wonder-worker from the first days of his priesthood.

Pius IX was one day accosted by an invalid who begged His Holiness to cure him. The saintly Pontiff smiled and replied: "My child, if you want a miracle, apply to Don Bosco in Turin. He has accomplished miracles of charity, and I should not be astonished if he worked others." Some of these "others" are related in this chapter. It is difficult to choose among so many, but certain ones are recorded, as they are characteristic of Don Bosco's way of answering the constant requests that all sorts of people brought to him.

Cures of illnesses speedily followed his blessing. But Don Bosco was always humbly eager to hide his personal part in the cure. Like the Curé of Ars, who "blamed" his cures on little St. Philomena, Don Bosco always claimed that Our Lady, Help of Christians, was the curer. There is the well-authenticated "Case of the Pills." A man was suffering from an incurable disease. His friends went to Don Bosco, who prescribed Confession and Communion. He also gave them a few pills to be taken, after the man had recited the "Hail, Holy Queen" three times a day for a certain period. The prayers were said; the pills were religiously taken, and the man recovered completely.

The drug-store man of the little town, with an eye to business, hastened to the Turin Oratory. He sought Don Bosco and begged for the formula of his wonderful prescription. Don Bosco blushed and told the drug-store proprietor that the pills were all consumed. But such an answer did not satisfy the man. He hastened back to the recovered man's house and was happy to find some of Don Bosco's pills that had not been taken. With these he sought his back room and eagerly analyzed the pills. They turned out to be made of ordinary bread. Another pharmacist made the same analysis. Bread pills! The whole town now was talking about those pills.

The man who had been cured traveled to Turin and thanked Don Bosco. He asked the man if the prayers to Our Lady had been faithfully said. Assured so, Don Bosco replied, "That was all that was needed."

Don Bosco was visiting one of the great city hospitals. In one of the wards was a woman in the last stages of consumption. She had stubbornly resisted the entreaties of the nuns and the Chaplain to make her peace with God. Her sad state was put before Don Bosco. He went to her bedside and after some brief conversation, suddenly changed his tone and said gravely:

"My good woman, I tell you in the name of God that in His infinite mercy He has granted you a few hours in which to think of the state of your soul. It is now four o'clock in the afternoon, and you have time to go to Confession and Communion, to receive Extreme Unction and the Papal Blessing. It is no use deluding yourself longer. To-morrow you will be in eternity."

Such direct words, coming from Don Bosco, had an

immediate effect on the poor creature. Meekly she asked that the Chaplain might be sent to her. He came and she died happily reconciled before the next dawn.

Another time, when Don Bosco was in Nice, on business connected with a newly established Oratory, he stopt to visit the Reverend Mother of the Convent of the Blessed Sacrament. She had been bedridden for over four years. Don Bosco was brought to her bedside. "Sister," was his introductory remark, "have you faith?" Somewhat surprised, the Reverend Mother faltered, "Indeed, I hope so, Father."

"Well, Sister, all is possible to those who believe. 'One good turn deserves another.' I visit you and you will visit me in return."

"I would gladly, please God, if I was able, but when will that be, Father?"

"This evening—the sooner a visit is acknowledged the greater the compliment."

Don Bosco bowed politely and left the room.

That afternoon when Don Bosco was walking in the street within sight of his Oratory, he stopt suddenly and said to his companion, "My friend, you have better eyes than I. Do you see anything opposite the Oratory?"

"Nothing, Don Bosco."

"No carriage?"

"No; Father."

"That's strange," said Don Bosco, seemingly talking to himself; "she has not yet come!"

After they had walked half a block, Don Bosco demanded: "Father, look again, please."

"For what?"

"For a carriage. Do you see a nun descending?"

The priestly companion looked and said. "Yes, a carriage has drawn up and two nuns are getting out."

When they came up to the Oratory, Don Bosco found the very grateful Reverend Mother of the Convent of the Blessed Sacrament awaiting him to return his morning visit.

At supper that evening the table conversation was largely on the bedridden Reverend Mother's cure. To persistent questions Don Bosco meekly remarked: "My friends, you see how good God and His Mother are!"

Don Bosco liked especially to cure the young. A typical case was that of Marie Stardero. This took place in May, 1869. She had been stone blind for two years. This May morning her aunt took her to the Church of Our Lady, Help of Christians. They prayed fervently before the Lady altar. Then they sought Don Bosco. "Take off the bandage," he ordered, and he turned the girl so that she faced a sunny window.

"Do you see the light?"

"No; Father. All is dark."

"Do you wish to see?"

"O my God! Indeed I do, Father." And Marie burst into tears.

"If God, through the intercession of Our Lady, Help of Christians, would restore your sight, would you use it to serve Him?"

"Can you doubt that, Father?"

"Well, my child, cease crying. Have confidence in Mary, Help of Christians, who has only to wish your cure to obtain it."

Don Bosco prayed silently. Then he reached into the pocket of his well-worn cassock and, taking out something, held it in his open palm. "For the glory of God and of Our Blessed Mother, say what I hold in my hand?"

Marie turned toward the direction of the priest's voice and suddenly exclaimed: "I . . . I . . . I . . . see!"

"What, my child?"

"A medal of the Blessed Virgin."

"And on the other side of the medal?" he questioned.

"A saint with a lily in his hand. That must be St. Joseph." At this moment Marie stretched out her hand to take the medal, but Don Bosco deliberately let it drop to the floor, where it rolled to a dark corner.

The weeping aunt attempted to recover it, but Don Bosco restrained her, saying: "No, let Marie look for it. That will prove if her sight is effectively restored."

The girl easily found and picked up the medal and then without waiting to thank Don Bosco, she began shouting with joy and followed by her aunt started to run home to her village of Vinovo. It is recorded that there was much excitement and little work in that quiet village all the rest of that day.

Often Don Bosco used these extraordinary answers to his prayers as a means to move another to repentance. His motto, "Give me souls, all else take," was at the back of this. For instance, there is a fair-sized town on the Gulf of Genoa, called Sampierdarena. The wife of a railway official was seized with a serious illness. She got worse and her doctor said she was going to die. The parish priest knew she and her husband were fallen-away Catholics, but when he heard of her condition he called at the house. The woman sent him word, "I do not wish to see you. If I go to Confession it will be to Don Bosco and to no other priest."

Don Bosco was in Turin, miles away, but when he heard

this answer, he said: "Poor soul, I will go and see her."

The woman claimed that the sight of Don Bosco gave relief from her pains. Willingly she made her confession to him.

"Now for Communion," said Don Bosco, "you better come to the church. I intend to remain here several days. I shall offer Mass and get my orphans to pray for you. Come one of these mornings and I shall give you Holy Communion myself."

The husband, hearing these words, was indignant. "Can't you see she is dying? The doctor tells me she will never leave that bed."

Don Bosco listened till the husband had finished and then he observed: "My friend, Our Lady, Help of Christians is all powerful." And he added, "If you pray to her also, we might probably obtain your cure with your wife's."

"Mine? But I am not ill!"

Don Bosco ignored this, but kneeling down he began to say the Hail Mary, Our Father, and the "Hail, Holy Queen." The husband almost unconsciously made the replies.

Don Bosco got up. "These prayers must be recited every day till Christmas." It was December 6. He hung a medal of Our Lady around the woman's neck and handed another to the husband.

A few days later, the husband and wife attended Don Bosco's Mass. He gave Holy Communion to the woman. When they came to the sacristy to see and thank him after Mass, Don Bosco remarked gently, "I now confidently await the second recovery." He looked smilingly at the man. That afternoon the husband went to Confession to

Don Bosco. Sampierdarena spoke of this double conversion for many days.

Naturally these cures spread Don Bosco's fame. At a conference of the clergy he was once asked point-blank about his miracles. His reply was, "No; Don Bosco does not work miracles, but I avow God is pleased sometimes visibly to recompense the generous benefactors of Don Bosco's undertakings." The clergy had to be content with this diplomatic reply.

One of those present that day remarked: "The simplicity of St. Vincent of Paul united with St. Francis of Sales' cordial affability, are characteristic of Don Bosco."

Among all these many "visible recompenses" many are the cures that Don Bosco effected on boys. We are inserting three characteristic ones here.

One day at Nice a seven-year-old boy was helped into his presence. The mother begged: "Don Bosco, please bless my child. See, he has never walked without the aid of crutches!"

Don Bosco raised his hand in blessing, saying: "Willingly do I bestow the blessing of Our Lady, Help of Christians." He patted the little fellow's cheek. Then he walked to the far corner of the parlor and turning, invited: "Come, my little friend, but without crutches. Let them fall. There, do not be afraid."

As the anxious mother attempted to help the boy, Don Bosco said: "Leave him alone. Do not give him your hand."

The boy hesitated a second and then as the mother said, "Do what the Father says," he timidly walked, step by step—the first unaided steps he had ever taken—till he fell into Don Bosco's outstretched arms.

"Now go back and get your crutches, my little friend."

The boy ran back, grabbed up the crutches and, followed by his wildly hysterical mother, rushed out to find Daddy. That family became another microphone through which was broadcast Don Bosco's name and fame.

In all his cures Don Bosco insisted on confidence in Our Lady's power. There is one boy who will never forget this insistence. This anecdote might aptly be entitled "The Boy Who Hesitated."

It seems that in May, 1869, Don Bosco was to visit his Oratory at Lanzo. Alas, confined to the Infirmary were seven boys, down with smallpox. Their isolation was intensified by the knowledge that they would miss all the festivities in the dining room in honor of their Oratory's Founder. These seven talked their misfortune over and they decided that Don Bosco should perform some of his cures on his own boys. So they begged the Infirmarian to give them their clothes and to tell Don Bosco that they wished to see him on a very important matter. Faithfully was their message carried to Don Bosco's ears and he came at once with the Superior of the Oratory.

"Please, Father, make us well," was the burden of the petition. That came from the seven beds.

Don Bosco told them to say a Hail Mary with confidence in Our Lady, Help of Christian's aid, and then he blessed them collectively.

"Have you confidence in Our Lady?" he asked.

"Yes, Father."

"Then, my boys, get up and join your companions in the good times below."

Don Bosco left the Infirmary. Six of the boys promptly got up and dressed; the seventh was doubtful about being cured and remained in bed. The six trooped down to the hall where prizes were being distributed. One of them heard his name read out as a premium winner. Somebody said he was sick in the Infirmary.

"I am not," was the indignant denial from the hall and the boy went up to receive his premium.

The school doctor was in the audience. He had not been informed of Don Bosco's intervention and he naturally examined his smallpox patients. The six were completely cured. The boy who hesitated about his cure was still ill. The disease ran its natural course and twenty days later he left the Infirmary. He was also cured of any hesitation he had in regard to Don Bosco's intercession with Our Lady.

That Don Bosco watched over his boys in his absence is well illustrated by this extraordinary incident. By the way, it is one of the rare times when swimming is mentioned in Don Bosco's biographies. For, unfortunately, swimming in Italy in the latter half of the last century was not as popular as in our own days in America. Father Victor Alasonatti was Superior of the Oratory at a time when Don Bosco was away to make his annual Retreat at Lanzo. In leaving he requested Father Alasonatti to write him frequently, telling how the boys were doing.

Such a letter was written to Don Bosco on a Sunday, narrating how edifying all the boys were. The answer came on Tuesday. Father Rua read it to the boys after night prayers in the dormitory. It took the place of the nightly little discourse. One who heard the letter read has given us this account of its contents:

I was very pleased [ran Don Bosco's letter] to learn that you are well, and still more that the boys are giving satisfaction. I know you tell me nothing that is not your heart's desire. It has always been my desire to assist you in this holy resolution and so it will be as long as Our Lord detains me on this earth. You tell me that you are superintending and that all is going well. You are not aware that on Sunday, perhaps just after you had written me such a glowing account, two boys left the Church during Vespers and went to Stura to swim, thus losing the evening service. One of them was even so unworthy a son of the Oratory as to make use of disgusting language. I gave him a reminder, however, which he will not forget in a hurry . . .

You say the prayers too quickly and consequently with little devotion. I even see four or five this evening and they are . . . (Don Bosco gave their names). These boys are meeting in the courtyard at the back of the house and are there holding a conversation by no means edifying.

Here Father Rua paused in the reading of the letter and observed: "I wished to ascertain if what Don Bosco said was true, or if it were merely a supposition on his part. I therefore must tell you this evening while we were at prayers I went to the place Don Bosco mentioned and there found the five culprits of whom he had spoken. They are now in my presence, listening to me, and will be a little surprised to know how the loving eye of Don Bosco discovered them from the Sanctuary of St. Ignatius at Lanzo."

This astonishing news was received in perfect silence. Father Francesia, who was a boy in the dormitory that evening has left us the rest of the story. He wrote:

I heard one of the boys confess to the assistant prefect of the dormitory, "Father, now I know who it was that struck me! Yesterday while I was in the water and was talking language that did not become a son of the Oratory, I felt a heavy blow upon my back as though someone had struck me with his fist. I got angry and shouted, 'Who struck me?'

"A soldier who was bathing a good distance off, said to me, 'You little idiot, you're miles away from everybody, and yet you ask who hit you. You've been dreaming.'

"But I am not dreaming. I can feel the bruise still. 'Then perhaps you hit against a rock,' said the soldier. I dropped the conversation, made for the bank, and ashamed of what happened, returned to the Oratory. Now I know whom to thank."

That memorable evening the boys talked of the extraordinary gifts that God had given to their Father.

We have kept for the end of this chapter an event that took place in 1849. That it is out of the ordinary is not the reason for its insertion here, but because it shows so well that great characteristic of Don Bosco, his shielding love for his boys that extended beyond the portals of death. There was a boy named Charles. He was about fifteen and the son of an innkeeper. Charles had frequented the Oratory at Valdocco regularly. He fell ill. The doctor warned the parents to get the priest and have him administer the Last Sacraments. Charles said he wanted to go to Confession to Don Bosco, who was his regular Confessor. The father went to Valdocco and learnt that Don Bosco was out of Turin and was not expected back for several days. The father told this news to his son. The boy became very sad at the news. Again and again he asked for Don Bosco. Messengers were dispatched to the Oratory, but they all brought back the same report—Don Bosco had not yet returned.

The disease grew worse rather than better and the parents sent in haste for the parish priest. He came promptly. The next day Don Bosco returned to Valdocco and the first thing he heard was that a dying boy, a former Oratory boy, had been calling for him. Don Bosco dropped everything and hastened to the inn. He met a waiter, who said: "You come too late, Father, Charles died about twelve hours ago."

"Not at all, my friend," replied Don Bosco; "he is just fast asleep and you think he is dead."

The waiter looked pityingly at the priest. Don Bosco said smilingly, "I bet you a pint that he is not dead."

Before the bet could be taken up, members of Charles' family came out, assuring Don Bosco of the death of Charles.

"Must I then believe it!" he exclaimed. "Let me go to see him."

Don Bosco was escorted to the darkened room, where the mother and aunt of the boy, weeping and praying, watched by the bedside. The body was already laid out for burial. According to custom, they had sewed it up in a winding sheet. The face was covered with a veil, and the dim light of a lamp was flickering gloomily by the bed.

Don Bosco approached. He gazed in silence at the shrouded figure for a long time. Then kneeling and praying fervently, he arose and blessing the body, called in a loud voice: "Charles, Charles, get up!"

At the sound of his voice the head began to move. Immediately Don Bosco removed the light and stept between the lamp and the bed. Then he lifted back the veil that covered the face of the boy. Charles, as though awakening from a deep sleep, opened his eyes wide. He stared around and cried: "What is the matter! What is the matter! Why am I tied up like this?"

The boy had turned his head till his gaze took in the priest standing by the bedside. The eyes shone with recognition. "Oh, Don Bosco! Oh, if you only knew! I've wanted to see you very much! Father, it is God Who has sent you here. I need your help badly."

Don Bosco leaned over the bed. "Well, now, my son, say all you wish. I am here to hear you."

"Ah, Don Bosco," Charles continued, "I should be lost for ever! In my Confession to the parish priest I was ashamed to tell a sin I committed some weeks ago. . . . I have just had a dream that struck me with terror. I dreamed I was on the brink of a horrible pit of flames. I was struggling with demons that strove to seize me. They were already on the point of pouncing on me to hurl me headlong into that bottomless pit, when a Lady stopped them, saying: 'Hold there! Charles has not yet been judged.' Then I heard your voice calling me by name and I woke up. Now, Father, I want to make my Confession to you."

While the boy wrapt in a winding sheet was talking, the mother and aunt, beside themselves at all that was going on in their presence, had been listening in stark terror. At a quick signal from Don Bosco they left the room to summon the rest of the family. Don Bosco soothed Charles and helped him to repair the bad Confession by a good one. While his hand was raised in Absolution the vanguard of the household arrived at the door.

The boy seeing his mother, cried out: "O Mother, Don Bosco has saved me from eternal damnation!"

She and the other relatives crowded around the bed. All noticed that though Charles moved his head and spoke, his body was stiff and cold—as cold as it had been when he had been prepared for his burial.

At length Don Bosco asked the boy: "Charles, my friend, now you are at peace with God. Heaven is open to you. Do you prefer to go there or stay with us?"

A breathless tenseness clamped on the witnesses as the boy in the winding sheet answered emphatically: "Oh, Don Bosco, I prefer to go now."

The priest raised his hand in benediction, saying: "*Au revoir*, Charles. Please God, we shall see each other in Heaven."

Charles' eyes closed. The faint flush of color receded from his cheeks. And the coldness of death spread up from the body.

Is it any wonder that the fame of Don John Bosco as a wonder-worker spread far and wide. The miracle worker of Turin was aptly called by Pius IX "The Treasure of Italy."

CHAPTER XV

TOWARD EVENING

THE *Salesian Bulletin* for December, 1884, contains this notice:

> Don Bosco feels deeply grateful to his Coöperators for charitable prayers, public and private, offered to God for his recovery. Those prayers have been heard, and he is now able to resume part of his former occupations. In testimonial of gratitude he celebrated Mass, the Feast of the Presentation of the Blessed Virgin, for all who kindly prayed for him. With all his children he supplicates the Lord to bless and prosper his Coöperators, and in this difficult and trying time avert all disaster from them and their families.

Don Bosco himself inserted this notice of his recovery. He had been so ill that his life was despaired of. All over the world prayers had been offered for his recovery. His time had not yet come.

Besides the demands that the now more than eighty Oratories and extensive South American Missions made on their Founder, there was another important work that was taking much of Don Bosco's later years. Some months before his death Pius IX had summoned his friend Don Bosco and had said to him, "You must build another basilica here in Rome. It will be the crowning work of your career; and to win the support of Providence, we will dedicate it to the Sacred Heart." Such a request coming from the Holy Father was a command for Don Bosco. Despite his failing health he immediately started the immense task.

Pius IX died soon after that audience. There is an interesting incident told of this period. Don Bosco was in Rome again at the time and because of his prominence and friendship with Italian officials he had been asked to approach the Government and learn if there would be any interference with the Conclave. The Prime Minister, Crispi, assured Don Bosco that there would be no Italian interference. Don Bosco hastened to the Vatican to inform the Cardinal Chamberlain, Cardinal Pecci, who did not know him personally. The two met in one of the Vatican corridors.

"Will Your Eminence allow me to kiss your hand?" humbly begged Don Bosco.

Busy with the many details of the coming Conclave, Cardinal Pecci demanded somewhat roughly: "Who are you?"

"I am a poor priest, and soon I hope not merely to kiss your hand, but also your feet."

"I forbid you to talk of such things," said the Cardinal.

"But Your Eminence cannot forbid me to ask of God that which is His Holy Will."

The Cardinal passed on and a few days later he was elected Pope and took the name of Leo XIII. The new Pope confirmed the command of his predecessor and encouraged Don Bosco to carry through the building of the Basilica of the Sacred Heart. So he went forth with the same sublime confidence that had animated him at the commencement of each of his great building projects.

The serious illness of 1884 only delayed his efforts. With his partial restoration to health he resumed his begging journeys. It takes faith to undertake the erection of a great church that will be six years in the building and will finally cost three million dollars. Yet this is what the aged Don Bosco accomplished. With directions in his saintly hands funds came in when the debts were due and all bills were paid.

He saw the solemn consecration of this splendid Basilica on May 14, 1887.

Those last years were years of consolation for Don Bosco. His name had grown to be synonymous with holiness and it was widely believed that Our Lord and Our Lady, Help of Christians, had given to his hands marvelous powers. Hence the lame and the halt and the blind, and those spiritually in a worse state, crowded the anterooms that led to his presence. His Salesian children had to watch to see that pieces of his cassock were not cut off. Once at Avignon, in France, the scissors of the pious had ruined his cassock. When Don Bosco noticed this he said ruefully, "If my cassock is so cut, at least I may expect a new one!"

Salesian foundations had sprung up in many cities of Italy, France and Spain. The Founder visited them. We have many accounts of the triumphant progress of "The Wonder-Worker of Turin." We take a picture that is typical of many another scene. It has added interest for us Americans as it is written by the Right Reverend Joseph Crimont, S.J., the Vicar Apostolic of Alaska. We may add in parenthesis that Bishop Crimont was in New York City while this life was being written. We talked with him, the only one we have met who had actually met Don Bosco and he confirmed the impression given below.

Here is Bishop Crimont's account of his meeting with Don Bosco:

On May 5th, 1883, Don Bosco went to Lille, France. The following morning he celebrated Mass in the Church of the Ladies of the Retreat. I was a young Subdeacon and I obtained the great privilege of serving his Mass. As soon as Don Bosco had crossed the threshold of the sacristy, the throng crowded all around him in order to ask his blessing and to kiss his hand. At every step a new crowd surrounded him, so much so that it took him a quarter of an hour to reach the foot of the altar and to begin his Mass.

I was next to him, enjoying the spectacle. But what a Mass it was! It was a unique spectacle! It was the Mass of a Saint and Don Bosco's face was brilliant in a supernatural way.

The next day, Don Bosco celebrated Mass in the Chapel of the Adoration, where the blessed Sacrament is perpetually exposed. The same enthusiasm, the same devotion of the preceding day were shown. I had the good fortune of assisting Don Bosco again, and I experienced the impression of his holiness as on the day before. When he reëntered the sacristy, I addressed myself to him. I told him that I was a young Jesuit in search of good health and that I wished to ask of him a favor. He asked me what was it that I wanted and I answered: "I wish to have sufficient strength to become fit to be sent to the Missions. I wish to be a missionary."

"My son," replied Don Bosco affably, "you shall receive the grace. I will pray to God for this purpose every day in my Thanksgiving after Holy Mass."

Bishop Crimont's memoir continues, "I recovered my health . . . and after my ordination in 1888, I was sent by my Superiors to the Missions of the Rocky Mountains and in 1894 I was transferred to Alaska."

During that journey to France just mentioned by Bishop Crimont, Don Bosco visited Paris. The usual crowds surrounded him. Don Bosco found time for each who sought him. A white-haired old gentleman came to the crowded antechamber. He took his place in line and waited three hours till his turn came. Many there recognized him, for he was a world-famous writer, and waiting there he must have observed his companions. He must have heard their eagerly expressed hopes that Don Bosco would cure themselves or some loved one. He could not escape noticing the joyous features of those who came out of the antechamber, where, from the lips of the humble Turin priest they had received words of comfort, and hope, and forgiveness.

When his time came this white-haired old gentleman went into the other room. We have Don Bosco's own account of that interview.

The gentleman said: "Above all, Don Bosco, I refuse to believe in the miracles which some persons are so loudly proclaiming about you."

"Sir," said Don Bosco, smiling gently, "tell me, what do you believe or admit with regard to a future life?"

"Oh, we need not lose time discussing that question!" was the flippant reply. "I will speak of the future when it arrives." Don Bosco looked kindly at this aged scoffer and asked: "If it is thus with you, what then do you hope for? Very soon the present will no longer be yours. Of the future you will not hear a word. Now, what is your hope?" The priest paused a moment, and then with gentle gravity, continued: "You are bound to think of the eternal future, my friend. You have but a short span of life, and if you profit by it to return to the bosom of the Church and to beg the mercy of God, you will be saved. If not, you will die as an unbeliever and as a reprobate."

The white-haired old gentleman hesitated for a moment before replying and then murmured something to the effect that the most advanced in philosophical thought have never been able to solve the problem of immortality or annihilation. He added, "Don Bosco, I will think over what you have been saying, and, if you will allow me, I will come back another day."

Saying this, he rose and grasped the hand of Don Bosco. Then he laid a visiting card on the table and in silence left the room. Don Bosco had not asked the old gentleman his name, but after he had departed, he picked up the card and read "Victor Hugo."

The third day after, the famous writer was back in the antechamber. Again he waited his turn and when it came he was admitted. This time he approached with outstretched hand and exclaimed: "Don Bosco, I was but playing a part the other day, when I spoke to you as I did. I want you to be my friend. I do believe in the immortality of the soul. I believe in God, and I hope to die in the arms of a Catholic priest, who will recommend my soul to its Creator."

What reply Don Bosco made to Victor Hugo has never been divulged. We can readily guess though that it had something to do with tempting Divine Providence and putting off till too late a reconciliation with God. It must have been disappointing to the proud intellect of one who had been "a god unto himself" these many years. Victor Hugo left the presence of Don Bosco. He lived a little over a year longer. There was no outward sign given, but it is known that Victor Hugo in his last moments was calling for a priest and calling in vain, because his Masonic "friends" would not heed that dying request. Poor Victor Hugo, may Blessed Don Bosco have aided him in those last precious moments!

Among the Oratories that Don Bosco founded which prospered exceedingly was the one at Barcelona, Spain. There are several remarkable incidents connected with this Spanish foundation that may well be related here. Back in December, 1880, Don Bosco had entrusted to one of his Salesians, Father Branda, the establishment of an Oratory in Utrera, Spain. As Father Branda was leaving Turin, Don Bosco remarked to him, "Father, in due time you will receive a letter for a wealthy lady of Barcelona, begging you to establish one of our Oratories in her city. This Institute is destined to have a magnificent future."

Father Branda always remembered this prediction and when a letter reached him in September, 1882, from a certain Doña Serra of Barcelona, offering him twenty thousand dollars toward the start of an Oratory, he accepted the offer. The Barcelona Oratory was opened early in 1884, and Father Branda was its first Director.

Several years later—to be exact the night preceding the feast of St. Francis of Sales, January 28, 1886—the Director was sleeping soundly when he heard his name called.

"Father Branda, Father Branda, get up and come with me." The voice was the voice of Don Bosco.

Father Branda, half awake, recognized the voice, but he thought to himself, "This is a good time for dreams. Don Bosco is in Turin and I want to sleep." With this he turned over and went to sleep again. He did not wake till the ringing of the morning rising bell. During the day he recalled what he thought was the vivid illusion of the previous night. But he gave it no further attention.

On the night of the octave of St. Francis' feast, February 5, the Director was roused from his sleep by hearing again, "Father Branda, Father Branda." He recognized the voice and sat up in bed. There was no lamp lit in his room, yet to his amazement he saw sharply outlined against the curtains of this alcove bed, the well-known silhouette of Don Bosco.

"Now you are awake," said the voice, "get up and dress."

"I shall come immediately," the Director replied. What his thoughts were are not recorded. When Father Branda was dressed, he pulled aside the bed curtain and there standing in his room was Don Bosco. And yet it was not Don Bosco. There radiated from his features a light that softly illuminated the whole room. Father Branda took hold of his Superior's hand and kissed it reverently.

Don Bosco said: "Your house goes on well enough. I am satisfied with all you do, but . . ." Don Bosco did not finish the sentence, for at that moment there appeared before them the faces of four of the boys of that Oratory. Pointing to the first, Don Bosco said: "Inspire in him greater prudence." Then Don Bosco's hand swept toward the other three boys. "Send them away as soon as possible. Do not show them mercy."

"When Don Bosco was pronouncing these expulsions," continues Father Branda's account of the bilocation, "his face appeared inflamed and wrathful. After this, at a signal from him, both of us went out of the room. I opened the door for him and followed him. We visited the two dormitories. I do not remember that Don Bosco opened their doors. I, on my part, did not open them, but followed him. On the way, the stairs and the dormitories were full of light as at daybreak and Don Bosco was going with bold steps, at a faster pace than he ordinarily used. Having returned to the Director's room, Don Bosco renewed his expulsion orders . . . and then the room was in darkness again. Father Branda groped his way to his writing desk and lit his lamp. The yellow glow showed him the familiar fixtures of his room. He glanced at his watch and saw it was close to three A.M. Sleep was out of the question, so he took up his Breviary and began to say his office till rising time. Then the Director as soon as possible said his Mass. He was still troubled how he could expel any boy without proof of some wrong-doing. In this disturbed state of mind Father Branda let several days pass till a letter came to him from Turin. It was written by Father Rua and in the letter he narrated how the evening before, while walking under the Oratory porches, Don Bosco had mentioned his making a nocturnal visit to Father Branda and he warned him to carry out the orders he had received that night.

Father Branda still could not bring himself to expel boys without proof. Next morning when he was saying his Mass, he had finished the prayers at the foot of the altar, when he seemed to hear an internal voice saying, "If you do not do what Don Bosco has commanded you, this is the last Mass you will celebrate!"

Father Branda needed no further urging. After Mass, he called the Prefect, Father Aime. They sent for the three boys and questioned them separately. Father Branda remarked that each assumed the identical shamefaced expression that he had when Don Bosco's hand had indicated him that night of his first visit. Each boy confessed enough to justify his expulsion and they packed their trunks and left the Barcelona Oratory that morning.

Don Bosco paid his first normal visit to this Barcelona Oratory in 1886. One afternoon while walking with Father Rua and Father Branda in the Oratory garden, Don Bosco pointed to a large field that was adjacent to the Salesian property. "Buy that ground for your garden."

"But, Don Bosco, I have no money," objected the prudent Father Branda.

"You doubt Providence!" exclaimed Don Bosco in surprise, "I never do." He continued, "Nevertheless, that field must be purchased." Then pointing to a neighboring garden, he added: "And buy that garden also and establish there a convent of Mary, Help of Christians, to educate young girls to be nuns for the missions."

Father Branda, still more amazed, protested: "My Father, I know the owner of that piece of property. He has so great a love for it that he will not part with it for less than forty thousand dollars."

Don Bosco listened patiently and then he said with an air of finality, "Father Branda, even though you have not a cent in the treasury, you must buy what I tell you. The Blessed Virgin desires there should be a home here for our Sisters. You will see how difficulties will vanish."

They did. Money came in most unexpectedly. The field was purchased. The owner of the garden died and his son sold the property to Father Branda on most reasonable terms. The Salesian Sisters opened their convent, as Don Bosco had predicted, in November of that same year.

About this time, at the request of his Salesians, Don Bosco let a celebrated physician, Dr. Combal, examine him. The doctor's report was, "It is said, and I quite believe it, that Don Bosco works miracles through the power of God, but the greatest miracle in my opinion is that he lives in this shattered state of health. He is like a garment worn out by use, which, if we wish to preserve, we must keep shut up in a wardrobe."

Another eminent doctor, Dr. Fissore of Turin University, visited Don Bosco. The doctor asked his age.

"I am seventy years old."

"Do not say seventy," objected the doctor who had just examined his heart, "but a hundred and fifty, for your life of continuous labor is equal to that of one who has lived a hundred and fifty years."

So Don Bosco returned to Italy, never to leave it again. He made the journey, as has been related, to Rome to witness the dedication of the Basilica of the Sacred Heart. It was a triumphant procession. Crowds gave him little leisure. When it was all over, Don Bosco returned to his beloved Valdocco Oratory where all his mighty works, now almost world-wide, had their humble beginnings.

How those last days were busy this pen picture, written by a Belgian gentleman, who visited Don Bosco in December, 1887, shows:

I had to go up numerous stairs, and at the top, in a very humble attic, I found Don Bosco. I remarked two splendid etchings there, attesting that if the object of the Institute was to educate artisans, artists too, belonged to it . . . I met Don Bosco's principal co-laborers, Father Rua, his vicar-general, and the other, his assistant, Father Durando . . . As the waiting room was full of visitors, Father Durando allowed me to pass into his [Don Bosco's] cell, where I was astonished to see evidences of great poverty. Many poor are better lodged and have better furniture than this eminent clergyman.

When at last I was to have the happiness of approaching Don Bosco my heart beat more quickly than in going before worldly potentates, reflecting that I was to meet one of those rare men whom God is pleased to raise up at certain times, to show what saints are and what they can achieve. Sanctity! How that word makes worldly people smile! Nevertheless, even from a human point of view, saints have had a great effect on individual lives and nations. . . . While thus reflecting my turn for admission came. I threw a rapid glance around the room, which was as miserable and poorly furnished as possible, and saw with emotion an old man, seated on a sofa, bent with age and the labors of a long apostolate. His failing powers no longer admitted of his standing up, but he raised his head, which was bent, and I could see his eyes, weak, but full of intelligent goodness.

Don Bosco spoke French fluently, slowly; but he expressed himself with remarkable clearness. He gave me a simple, dignified, and cordial welcome. I was much touched by an aged, almost dying man, unceasingly invaded by visitors, evincing such sincere, sympathetic interest in all. . . . With Don Bosco the sword had cut the scabbard, but what strength of mind still existed in the weakened body! With what a tone of regret he deplored that feebleness which prevented him from actively directing his numerous

works! Who more than he is entitled to intone with
confidence the Canticle of holy Simeon, "Now, Lord,
dismiss your servant in peace?"

So ends the pen picture, but we carry away from this
Belgian gentleman's words a picture of Don Bosco's last
days, when "the sword had cut the scabbard" and his vital
sanctity drew all to him.

Don Bosco's favorite blessing of these visitors was
to hand them a medal of his dear Lady, Help of Christians, and say, "May the Blessed Virgin protect you and
guide you to Heaven!" Or, if the kneeling one was a
priest, "God grant that you may lead many souls to Him!"

His last circular to his Salesian Coöperators is a long
letter, filled with the meekness of St. Francis of Sales and
the zeal of St. Vincent of Paul. Its final paragraph
breathes Saint John Bosco.

> In conclusion, I must tell you my health declines
> visibly; and I foresee the day approaches when I am
> leaving you, and when I shall have to pay my tribute
> to death, and descend into the grave. Should my
> presentiments be fulfilled, and this letter be the last
> one you receive from me, I recommend to your charity
> all the works which God has deigned to entrust to
> me during the last fifty years; the Christian education
> of youth, ecclesiastical vocations, and foreign mis-
> sions: I also particularly recommend poor, desolate
> children to your care, who were always dear to my
> heart, and who I hope will be, through the merits
> of Our Savior Jesus Christ, my crown and my joy in
> Heaven. Now I invoke God's benediction on you;
> may He deign to pour His most precious blessings on
> you and yours; if my prayer is heard, you will have

happy lives, full of merit, crowned on the day God fixes, with the death of the just. With this object, the Salesians and all pupils of our institutes unite their prayers, daily with mine, and through the intercession of Our Lady, Help of Christians, and of St. Francis of Sales, we have a firm and sweet hope of being all united in eternal bliss. Have the charity to pray in your turn for me, who am, with the deepest gratitude, well beloved Coöperators,

Your humble, devoted servant,

JOHN BOSCO, Priest.

Turin, December 8th, 1887.

CHAPTER XVI

JANUARY 31, 1888

THE knowledge that the reward "exceeding great" is close at hand must be a distracting thought to the Beloved of God. That knowledge was now Don Bosco's. In October of 1887 he had gone to the Seminary at Foglizzo and given the habit to over a hundred young Salesians. After the ceremony he had whispered to Father Rua, "My son, remember that you will have to perform this ceremony next year. This is the last time I will do it."

On another occasion in that Fall he told the Director of the Valdocco Oratory, "Hasten to ask the permit for my grave," adding pleasantly, "for if you do not, when I am dead I shall have myself carried to your room."

His last visit to his well-beloved Church of Our Lady, Help of Christians, was on December 4. It was the occasion of the Departure Ceremony of a band of Salesian Missionaries, leaving for Ecuador. Everybody present knew that another well-beloved one would be leaving for a farther country shortly after these departing missioners.

As Don Bosco was being assisted back to his quarters, he was told that Father Louis Deppert lay seriously ill in a room on the second floor. "I will see him," said Don Bosco. About to leave the room, Don Bosco remarked: "Courage, Father Louis, your hour is not yet come. On this bed on which you lie, another is to die before you."

This prophecy was accurately fulfilled, for when Don

Bosco took to his bed, it was found too narrow and the doctors ordered a more comfortable one to be brought. Father Deppert had recovered and his bed was brought into Don Bosco's room. So it was on the bed formerly occupied by Father Louis that Don Bosco died.

On December 17, some thirty penitents waited patiently in the anteroom for their chance to see Don Bosco. It was an evident strain on him and when an impatient Salesian son advised that the waiting group be dismissed, he said gently, "No, let them come in. It is the last time." As always he gave to each his undivided attention. These were the last Confessions he heard. In this connection it might be mentioned that with the exception of the Curé of Ars, Saint John Vianney, no priest in these latter days is said to have heard as many Confessions as Don Bosco.

The break in Don Bosco's health came shortly before Christmas, 1887. On the Eve, his Confessor, Father Giacomelli, came to see Don Bosco. Some of the Salesians recalled a prediction of their Founder, made three years before when Father Giacomelli was very ill. "Be of good heart and fear not. Don't you know that you will have to assist me at the hour of my death?"

Bishop Cagliero, just back from his vast Patagonian Missions, brought his spiritual father Holy Viaticum in solemn state. Humbly Don Bosco said to those of his sons who stood about the bedside, "Help me to receive Our Lord worthily."

The news spread rapidly that the Saint of Turin was dying. Public and private prayers were offered. Most fervent were the prayers of the countless boys who owed their all to Don Bosco. When he rallied with the dawn of the New Year, Don Bosco attributed his rally to "the prayers of our good boys."

Bishop Cagliero asked Don Bosco if it would be all right if he went to Rome to pay his visit to the Holy Father.

"You will go afterwards, my son."

The Bishop persisted: "But, Don Bosco, if I go before the Feast of St. Francis of Sales (January 29) can I go without fear?"

"Yes, yes; you will go, my son. You will do much good. But afterwards."

The rally, as everybody knew in his heart, was only temporary. By the twenty-fifth of January Don Bosco was again dangerously ill. He kept his cheerful humor to the last.

> Sometimes [wrote Father Rua, soon to be his successor] when Don Bosco would not be able to speak, he would question those who stood by his bedside, "Do you know where there is a factory that makes bellows?" To their surprised inquiries, he would reply, "I need a new bellows within here." He would indicate his chest. "My old bellows does not wish to serve me any longer. I need to change my bellows and so I am not able to speak as strongly and as freely as I should."

Once Bishop Cagliero exhorted him to remember the sufferings of Jesus, unable to move on His Cross. Don Bosco replied, "Yes; that is what I am always doing."

Father Sala, to encourage him, suggested, "My Father, you must feel contented at the thought of having established at the cost of so much labor and fatigue the Salesian Society and extended its houses to other continents?"

"Yes," said Don Bosco, "what I have done, I have done for God . . . and I would I had been able to do more . . . but my sons will do that, led as they are by God and protected by Our Lady, Help of Christians."

Don Bosco asked his watchers to suggest to him some pious ejaculations, and from time to time he would turn with difficulty in the direction of the Sanctuary and make the Sign of the Cross. On January 28, before receiving Holy Communion for the last time. Afterwards he dropped end!" And then to Father Bonetti, "Tell my boys that I will be awaiting them all in Paradise!"

The next day, the feast of his lifelong patron and favorite saint, St. Francis of Sales, Don Bosco received Holy Communion for the last time. Afterwards he dropt off into a sleep and remained so for the entire day. Elsewhere in the house, as were Don Bosco's wishes, the feast of the Patron of the Salesians was celebrated, but with saddened gayety. He remained in this drowsiness and only aroused himself when some one spoke of Paradise or of his soul.

Father Bonetti whispered to him the ejaculation, "Mary, Mother of Grace, protect us from the enemy," and Don Bosco replied, "and receive us at the hour of death." From time to time he was heard to murmur, "Mother! Mother!"

At ten on the morning of January 30, Bishop Cagliero intoned the Litany of the Dying, at which time the room was crowded with Don Bosco's sons. The doctors had said that that evening, or before dawn next morning, the release would come. The news spread quickly throughout the Salesian Houses in Turin. All who were able hastened to the Valdocco Oratory. Father Rua permitted these to file past the bed and kneel and kiss the hand of

their father. Silently they formed hushed groups in the
private chapel and came into the room one by one.

Their final look at Don Bosco showed him in a small
bed, with his head raised up and a little inclined toward
his left shoulder and supported by the pillows. He was
calm, his eyes half closed and his worn hands extended.
On his breast there was a crucifix and placed at the foot
of the bed there was a violet stole, the symbol of his fruitful priesthood.

Silently these spiritual children approached one by one,
knelt for a moment, and sorrowfully kissed the hand that
had been raised so many times to bless or absolve them.
Then privileged ones among Don Bosco's boys—some successful workmen and fathers of families, others still boys
in the Turin Oratories—knelt for that last still blessing.
How many memories of affection and care and hope must
have arisen in their bosoms as they gazed on their greatest
benefactor. Each had some medal or rosary or crucifix
that he wished the now helpless hand of good Don Bosco
to touch, that it might be cherished as a sacred memorial.
All afternoon these men and boys sought Don Bosco and,
even after darkness fell, more came. A saint was going
to his reward; a saint, who had been to each of them a
dear father.

That evening a cable arrived from Ecuador, which
announced the safe arrival of the last batch of Salesian
missioners—the ones whom Don Bosco had blessed in
December. Father Rua hastened to whisper the good news
into the ear of Don Bosco. He opened his eyes and looked
toward Heaven.

The death watch continued. Midnight struck. All but
Father Rua and several of the Superiors retired. Don

Bosco passed the dark silent hours motionless, except for his heavy sighing. The Divine Office of that night agreed with his slow agony. It was the Office of the Prayer of Jesus in the Garden.

January 31, 1888, had come. Shortly before two o'clock a change occurred. Father Rua put on his stole and resumed the Prayers for the Dying. The other Salesians were recalled. Quickly the room filled. Bishop Cagliero took the stole from Father Rua and, kneeling at the right side of the bed, whispered huskily into the ear of Don Bosco, "Father, your sons are here. We beg pardon for all the displeasure which, through our fault, you must have suffered. As a signal of pardon and your paternal love give us your Benediction once more. I will lift up your hand and pronounce the formula of Benediction."

Gently Bishop Cagliero took up the blessed hand; helpless now to raise itself. It rose and fell and crossed, while he invoked the protection of Mary, Help of Christians, on Don Bosco's sons present and scattered over the continents of the world.

At three that morning arrived a telegram from the Vatican. It was from Leo XIII, sending "from the depths of our heart" the Apostolic Benediction "to our beloved son, Don Bosco, seriously ill."

Another hour and a half passed and then the Bishop read the *"Proficiscere"*—the "Depart, O Christian soul, out of this sinful world, in the name of God . . . of the Blessed Virgin Mary . . . of the Confessors and all the Saints of God; let peace come to thee this day, and let thy abode be in holy Sion; through Christ Jesus, Our Lord. Amen."

Singularly appropriate words for this happy death!

Don Bosco yet lingered. It seemed as though he wished to hear for the last time the sweet bells of his near-by Church of Our Lady, Help of Christians, ring out the Angelus. They did. The labored breathing ceased. There was a free breath and an easy one.

"Our Don Bosco is dying!" a voice called out. It was true. He had lived seventy-two years, five months, and fifteen days.

Saint Don Bosco could not have remained long in Purgatory; if he ever saw the inside of it. There are several reasons for this pious belief. At Nyas, France, there was a parish priest who had spoken to Don Bosco, back in 1886, about a scientist of his parish. This man had neglected his religion for several years, causing considerable scandal in the neighborhood.

Don Bosco was wrapt in thought for a few moments and then he said, "Père, do not lose hope. Let us both pray to Mary, Help of Christians, and she will obtain this conversion."

Let this parish priest tell the sequel:

> On the morning of January 31st, 1888, as I was sitting in my room, I looked up and to my surprise beheld Don Bosco standing before me.
>
> "You here, Don Bosco!" I exclaimed.
>
> "Yes," he replied with his characteristic smile, "I have come to tell you that Our Lady has granted your request."
>
> "I am very grateful to her and to you," I said, "but why did you come here without letting me know? I should have wished to . . ."
>
> Here I stopped, for Don Bosco had disappeared and I was left alone. I thought I must have been

dreaming, till later that same morning I heard of Don Bosco's death.

There was a little sister in a Turin convent who was sick abed. Her family had done many charitable things for Don Bosco and his boys. When this nun heard that Don Bosco was dying she said to herself, "I will have my mother go to him and recommend me to his prayers."

So she asked her mother to go to Valdocco. Again we will let this sister relate the sequel:

> On the morning of January 31st, while the whole Community were in the Chapel, after a troubled night I fell asleep. Then I heard some one call out, "O Sister Philomena, what is the matter?"
>
> There was Don Bosco standing at the foot of my bed. He was wearing his usual cloak, raised on his arm and he was holding his biretta in his right hand. He was as young, happy, and as lively as when I had seen him so many times in our house, during my childhood.
>
> "Oh, Don Bosco," I cried out in delight, "Has my mother spoken to you about me? I am so disgusted and so weak that I am not able to do anything good."
>
> "I know that your mother wanted to come to me, but she was not able," replied Don Bosco. "You see, when I was in this world, I was able to do little good for you and your family. But now that I am in Paradise, I can do much more good. . . . Get up now, my child, God is with you."

Sister Philomena obeyed and joined the rest of her surprised Community in the Chapel.

Naturally Don Bosco did not lose interest in any of his boys. On the following morning, February 1, one of these boys lay dying in the Valdocco Oratory Infirmary. His mother was with him. Suddenly he looked up and his eyes were held by some attractive object by the door.

"Mother," he cried, "did you see him?"

"Who?" the mother asked.

"Don Bosco!"

"Surely not! Good Don Bosco is dead and his body is lying in the church."

"Well, I saw him," the boy insisted. "He came to tell me that in three days he will take me with him to Heaven."

The mother pooh-poohed the idea, but as she saw it persisted in the boy's mind, she resolved to have him removed from the Infirmary to the Hospital of the Sisters of Charity. She did two days later in the midst of a heavy snowstorm. When he was placed in a hospital bed, the boy said to the Sister on the ward, "Please may I receive Holy Communion to-morrow morning?"

"Surely, dear," said the Sister, "you must be one of Don Bosco's boys. They are all alike! As soon as any of them are admitted to our hospital they ask at once for Confession and Communion."

The boy interrupted, "I am going to die very soon, Sister. To-morrow Don Bosco will come for me."

"No, no," protested the mother, "do not believe him! He is still under that delusion!"

The next morning the Chaplain brought Our Lord to the boy. With evident joy he received Him. The mother kept her vigil by the bedside. At five that afternoon the boy woke from his sleep. His eyes opened to their widest. "See, Mother! I told you so! Here he is! Here he is! Oh, come quickly!"

It had been no delusion. Saint Don Bosco had but reversed his usual process. Instead of seeing his boys safely to the gates of eternity, now he was escorting them through.

CHAPTER XVII

SAINT JOHN BOSCO

AT his going Home, Don Bosco was Superior General over two hundred and fifty Salesian Communities. In these houses were one hundred and thirty thousand children, increasing daily in wisdom and age and grace—future useful citizens of their country and loyal subjects of their God.

It has been estimated that up to 1888 about twenty-five hundred of Don Bosco's boys had listened to the higher call that led up the aisle to the altar. Countless others since—boys and girls—have kindled to his spirit and have followed in his footsteps, deeming their days well spent, instilling Christ's knowledge into Christ's less fortunate little ones.

Rome, that moves with the slowness of the centuries, quickened her pace to lay wreaths of bay on the humble head of John Bosco. Leo XIII started the Process for his Cause within twenty-nine months after his death. Pius X declared him Venerable in July, 1907. He was Beatified by Pius XI in 1929 and that day his native Castelnuovo d'Asti changed its name to Castelnuovo Don Bosco and felt itself honored by the change. Then in 1934—a unique distinction, for it was the very Feast of the Resurrection, Easter Sunday—the honors of Canonization came to plain John Bosco. St. Peter's, Vatican City, found its immense capacity too small to hold the vast congregation, drawn from his native Italy and the world, that came to honor this most modern Blessed Friend of Youth. The Bull, proclaiming him worthy of the honors of the altars of the Universal Church was read in the presence of the Sovereign Pontiff, Pius XI, who had declared, "We have seen this man, John Bosco, face to face; we have talked with him. . . . In our opinion, he was one of those men who leave the mark of their genius wherever they are. . . ." Cardinals and Bishops, Generals of Religious Orders and Congregations, Princes of the Blood, a resplendent Diplomatic Corps, priests, people and many boys knelt when the illuminated painting of Saint John Bosco was uncovered for the first public veneration. That Easter evening His Holiness made his solemn entry into St. Peter's to kneel in prayer before the relics of his friend, the latest Saint. According to custom the crowds roared their welcome to Christ's Vicar and they varied their acclaim by shouting, "Long Live Don Bosco's Pope!"

Between the dates of Saint John Bosco's death and canonization, 1888-1934, lies an interesting comparison. Redemptorists called their Founder, Alphonsus Liguori, Saint after fifty-two years. Jesuit sons waited sixty-five years to see their Founder, Saint Ignatius Loyola, ascend the altars of the Catholic Church. The Vincentians' Founder, Vincent de Paul, was canonized seventy-seven years after his death. But Salesians saw their Don Bosco win this crowning honor within forty-six years.

The lights on the dome of St. Peter's were a fitting symbol of that imperishable crown that Saint John Bosco, boy worker and boy lover, will wear for all eternity. For the little farmer boy of Becchi, born on that last century day when a crushed Bonaparte was being borne to his exile on bleak St. Helena's isle, has come into the real honors of a true Conqueror.

When you go to Washington, make it your business to visit the Corcoran Art Gallery. Climb the main stairs and there, arresting your attention, is a statue of Napoleon. He sits alone in his chair, lost in thought. It's easy to read his thoughts. On his lap, half spread out, is a map of Europe. He had been gazing on that map. Names of countries that he won . . . battles that he lost . . . Waterloo . . . stare up at him like sullen ghosts. But he has forgotten them now. His fading eyes are staring into the setting sun—into eternity. For the sculptor has depicted the dying Napoleon—a Conqueror about to render an account of his conquests to God. Gaze long on that dying Napoleon and the sermon that he preaches to those who will hear. Then forget him.

Turn your mind to another statue that stands in honor before the Turin Basilica of Mary, Help of Christians. It is not a statue, but a group. It's hard to think of any artist depicting boy-loving John Bosco alone in solitary state. John Bosco and his boys are there in heroic-sized bronze. His hand is resting characteristically on several poor boys. Other boys—at work, at school, at noisy play —are below the central group.

Each of the sculptors has amply summed up the character of his subject. Both men realized their ambition. Maréchal Foch said of Napoleon, "He never learnt the things of the spirit are stronger than the most powerful armies." Pius XI said of Don Bosco, "In the life of this Servant of God, the supernatural became as the natural and the extraordinary appeared ordinary."

Fit epitaph for Bonaparte! Fit epitaph for John Bosco!

Both are now in God's eternity. One personified selfishness on a continental scale. He saw in boys fine bodies to fashion into fine soldiers of his Empire and so he used them. The other personified fatherly love on a world-wide scale. He saw in boys immortal souls. For these immortal souls he toiled and begged and fathered. Ah! vaster than the crowds that throng St. Peter's are these young souls—his crown and his joy and his reward exceeding great—who yesterday, to-day, and endless to-morrows call this modern Conqueror, blessed, twice blessed, Saint John Bosco!